WINNING PLAY IN TOURNAMENT AND DUPLICATE BRIDGE

other books by Fred L. Karpin

THE POINT-COUNT SYSTEM
OF BIDDING IN CONTRACT BRIDGE

THE PLAY OF THE CARDS

PSYCHOLOGICAL STRATEGY IN CONTRACT BRIDGE

HOW TO PLAY SLAM CONTRACTS

THE COMPLETE BOOK OF DUPLICATE BRIDGE (CO-AUTHOR)

WINNING PLAY IN TOURNAMENT AND DUPLICATE BRIDGE

HOW THE EXPERTS TRIUMPH

by Fred L. Karpin

with a Foreword by Alfred Sheinwold

THE NEW AMERICAN LIBRARY

FIRST PRINTING

PUBLISHED BY THE NEW AMERICAN LIBRARY, INC.
1301 AVENUE OF THE AMERICAS, NEW YORK, NEW YORK 10019
PUBLISHED SIMULTANEOUSLY IN CANADA BY
GENERAL PUBLISHING COMPANY, LTD.
LIBRARY OF CONGRESS CATALOG CARD NUMBER: 68-19535
PRINTED IN THE UNITED STATES OF AMERICA

ACKNOWLEDGMENTS

I am most deeply indebted to Alphonse ("Sonny") Moyse, Jr., the former publisher and editor of *The Bridge World,* for permission to reprint various deals which were selected from *The Bridge World.* Without his permission, this book would have been an impossible one to write; many of the topflight players of the 1930's and 1940's have passed away, leaving no living examples of their magnificent talents, thoughts, utterances, and practical feats at the bridge table, except those chronicled in *The Bridge World.*

I also wish to thank the following world-renowned authorities and players for having given me permission to reprint verbatim articles which were written by them in *The Bridge World:* B. Jay Becker, Richard L. Frey, Lee Hazen, Peter Leventritt, Theodore Lightner, Howard Schenken, and Alfred Sheinwold.

And to the many expert bridgeplayers—both living and dead—who are mentioned in this book, I owe a debt of gratitude. Although they had nothing to do with the actual writing of this book, some of the deals that confronted them in top-echelon combat have been assimilated into this text as illustrations of the functioning of the expert mind in the crucible of play. As a result of their real-life contributions, I was spared the time and effort of "building up" laboratory hands to describe the thought processes of the expert as he prepares and proceeds to play out a hand. My appreciation and thanks are hereby recorded.

Fred L. Karpin
October, 1967

This book is dedicated to the memory of my good friend, the late Albert H. Morehead. It was he who first suggested that I write a book depicting "the functioning of the expert mind." This text is the product of his suggestion.

FOREWORD

To play a game well may be a sign of an ill-spent life, an observation that you probably did not expect to see in the foreword to a book on bridge. As a friendly, philanthropic soul I merely wish to provide you with the best of all excuses for playing bridge the way you do.

Actually, there is nothing difficult about playing first-class bridge. Not a single concept of the game is profound; not a single maneuver is beyond the brainpower of an intelligent adolescent. The sole advantage of the expert is that he has developed the ability to think his simple thoughts without wondering where he parked the car, or what he is going to do about those bothersome accounts receivable, or whether the blonde kibitzer is any better than she ought to be.

That is all, but it is a lot.

At the end of the first world championship, held in Bermuda in 1950, the captain of the British team congratulated the victorious Americans not for their brilliance but for "a remarkable feat of concentration." It was a tribute that one player of world championship caliber could realistically pay to another.

By one of the sad ironies of life concentration is easier for the expert than for the average player. The expert is so accustomed to thinking in the right direction that he usually sees the point of a hand at the first or second attempt. The average player in the same situation will think of a dozen other bridge ideas before the key feature of the hand occurs to him. After a few hands, the average player is exhausted; the expert has not even worked up a mental sweat.

The great value of a book like this is that the average player sees what the expert has thought in a variety of puzzling bridge situations. As in any book by Fred Karpin, the examples are well-chosen and clearly presented—so that the student will meet similar situations in actual play and should recognize them when he meets them (rather than a few hours later).

If you really want to play better bridge, you will do more than enjoy these hands passively. You will wonder when you last met a hand of the same type. You will speculate on methods of recognizing hands of the same nature when you meet them disguised during the course of play. Such thoughts are simple, but time-consuming.

Few will actually bother to do this, since very few of us have ever acquired a taste for work. If you are one of the few, this book will open doors for you. If you are one of the many, you can still enjoy reading about the few. And you can comfort yourself with the reflection that you have better things to do with your time.

—Alfred Sheinwold

CONTENTS

INTRODUCTION

All of the deals presented in this book arose in top-flight games, in the big leagues of the bridge world. They were all played by renowned experts. In my opinion, the experts' adroit handling of these deals warrants placing them on a pedestal, for present and future generations of bridgeplayers to admire and to strive to emulate.

The purpose of this book is to give the reader an insight into how the mind of the expert functions in the play of the cards; and to illustrate how his playing power derives its strength not only from his mastery of correct technique, but also from his practical imagination and from the apparent simplicity of his play, wherein there frequently lurks some diabolical scheme designed to ensnare a less-expert, or gullible, opponent, or to outwit him.

In the majority of situations—in both real life and in this book—the expert succeeds in trapping his prey. On occasion, however, he fails, for the intended victim either sees the pitfall and avoids it, or never sees it and, through blissful ignorance, staggers home successfully.

It is part of Navy tradition that when a ship and its complement have gone through a period of tribulation and have come through with honor and glory, the commanding officer will salute them with the commendation: "Well done!" It is my belief that as the reader perceives the exploits of our bridge heroes parade in review, he will rise to his feet and applaud them with a "Well done!" for their achievements.

—Fred L. Karpin
October, 1967

DECLARER'S PLAY

chapter **1**

DECLARER'S PLAY: PROLOGUE

The subject of declarer's strategy and tactics is a colossal one. It encompasses such a myriad range of diverse types of situations that it cannot be classified or covered adequately by stereotyped formulas. Each hand, no matter how simple it may appear to be, or how similar it may appear to be to some apparently analogous previously-encountered deal, requires original planning and special individual treatment. In other words, each "newly-born" deal is a world unto itself, and is governed by its own set of laws; and within the limitations of the cards themselves, the success or failure of a contract depends on an intelligent, analytical handling of the problems indigenous to that deal. Hence, if the optimum result is to be attained, the thinking process must become—and forever remain—the first line of offense (or defense, as the case might be).

In view of the manifold ramifications inherent in declarer's play, and the impossibility of categorizing them into types or patterns of behavior that the student of the game can memorize and bring into judicious use when the occasions for their employment arise, the approach of this text will be *to analyze the thought processes of the expert player as he prepares and proceeds to play out a hand.* If the reader studies the step-by-step development of these thought processes, he will be able to deduce therefrom the proper mind-set for skillful play. This mind-set he must understand and absorb, for it is the prime component of the equipment essential to the correct resolution of the problems that are continually confronting all the declarers of the world.

Contract bridge came into being in 1925 and was fathered by

Harold S. Vanderbilt. Since its birth, numerous systems of bidding have been devised, each having specialized innovations and divergent techniques, and each claiming that it was more "scientific" than its predecessors had been. Each new system was designed with the end in mind of reducing the vagaries of chance to a minimum. In short, it was the hope of the "system-makers" that skill would become more predominant, at the expense of luck, resulting in the creation of better players.

Some of the earlier systems were the Vanderbilt Club System, the Two-Club System, the Reevue System, the One-Two-Three System, the Official System, the Culbertson Approach-Forcing System, and One-Over-One System—and probably dozens of others. With the passage of time, scores of additional *new* systems, derived from the impact of revised experiences at the bridge tables, were created to captivate the minds of contract-bridge devotees: the Goren System, the Roth-Stone System, the Kaplan-Sheinwold System, the Bulldog System, the Stayman System, the Schenken System; and, of the past decade, the Italian Systems, the proponents of which have compiled an amazing record of successes in international competition. All of the above systems were created by Americans except the Italian Systems. These do not include the many systems of foreign origin that were developed in England, France, Austria, Sweden, etc.

Systemically speaking, it is my opinion that we haven't even scratched the surface with respect to unearthing, or manufacturing, systems of effective bridge bidding. Systems will perish as experience negates their assumed validity; and new systems, incorporating the sound tenets and principles of the superseded ones, will arise to take their place. The latter, too, will eventually pass away, leaving behind the accumulated guiding and workable principles as a heritage to the future generations of systems. To even faintly suggest that any contemporary or not-too-distant future system is the final word on "scientific" bridge bidding is to court ridicule by ignoring history. As has been amply demonstrated in the forty years since the birth of contract bridge, no system incapable of daily modification, alteration, and growth is worthy of acceptance and survival, and inevitably it either withers away or is discarded as technologically unfit. The game of contract—and the systems that strive for optimum efficiency—will change as its players, fortified by experience, improve their bidding techniques and allow greater scope to their imaginations.

In summary, we are still millenniums away from someone uttering the final word on contract-bridge bidding, if it ever will be uttered. Should the time ever come when bidding theory and systems of bidding will cease to be reinforced by additional knowledge, we will be forced to say "adieu" as we reluctantly search for a new game to conquer and master.

In contrast to bidding theories and systems of bidding, where change has always occurred and will continue to take place, the theory of "declarer's play of the hand" has remained virtually unchanged from the day the game was created. And in the future, as in the past and the present, the theory of declarer's play will remain immutable. There is a sound reason for this apparent paradox.

Basically, the play of the cards is governed by mathematical probabilities. From the viewpoint of the declarer, there is—and has been—just one proper way of playing any given hand. For example, to use a rather naïve illustration, suppose you are in a grand-slam contract at spades and hold the following trump combination: Dummy—J 10 9, You—A Q 8 7 6 3. For all time—in the absence of any external clues—the proper play is to lead the jack and finesse. Anyone who plays the ace instead, hoping to catch a singleton king, must inevitably be a losing bridgeplayer, both now and in his reincarnation a thousand years hence. Thus, as far as declarer is concerned, a good book on the technical aspects of declarer's play written ten, twenty, thirty, or forty years ago* will be just as sound and practical as a good book written today, or from here on. With respect to declarer's play, there are no longer any unexplored areas. With the passage of time and the impact of cumulative experiences, the universe has been conquered and maximum efficiency attained, at least in theory.

In contrast to declarer's play, the defenders' play is a horse of another color. If declarer's play could be considered to be in the state of manhood, defenders' play would still be in the state of infancy. This would be attested to by all bridgeplayers, from the top-flight expert down through the rankest neophyte. All of them would

* A prime example would be Louis H. Watson's *Play of the Hand at Bridge*, published in 1934.

also agree that of the three departments of bridge—bidding, declarer's play, and defenders' play—the most difficult to master is defensive play. And, going further, there is unanimous concurrence in the oft-repeated assertion that more mistakes are made in defense than in either of the other two departments of bridge. There are two major reasons accounting for this deficiency in the techniques of defense.

First, when declarer is playing out a hand, he sees the twenty-six cards that belong to him and his partner, the dummy. He knows exactly how many cards of each suit his side possesses, what the quality of the cards is, and what his specific future problems are. In brief, he knows his *precise* strength and weakness, and is thereby enabled to deploy his resources in an intelligent manner while waging his campaign. The defenders, on the other hand, do not see their twenty-six cards, but only the thirteen that each of them holds. Thus, the defenders' task is automatically much more difficult, since each must try to figure out, or deduce, or imagine—or guess—what his partner is holding. Of course, they also have signals available to them, about which more later in Part II of this book, "Defenders' Play."

And secondly, it is an established fact that "scientific development" in the field of defense has lagged far behind the scientific development of bidding methods and techniques of declarer's play. There are relatively few guiding principles to point the way to proper defense. As a consequence, a defender is frequently on his own because the pattern of correct defense varies greatly from deal to deal. Many diverse defensive situations arise where there exists no precedent to take a defender by the hand and lead him to the desired objective. In these situations, judgment and/or imagination must operate independently of any established governing law.

As was stated a few paragraphs back, the subject of defensive play—and the functioning of the expert mind therein—is discussed and illustrated later on in this text. For the present, let us concern ourselves with declarer's play, and, in this role, the functioning of the expert mind.

Here are three deals that arose in the adolescent years of contract bridge. They were each played in tournaments: the first in 1929, the second in 1931, and the third in 1935. Sociologically, we would tend to view these ancestors of ours as "primitives," but on examination of their play I am sure there will be unanimity in the viewpoint that they were our equals in every respect. In the first two deals, the narration is done by the actual declarer.

Deal 1:

Willard Karn* is the South declarer and narrator. The deal was played in 1929.

"As a practical example of declarer's thought processes, I have chosen one of the hands I played in a tournament.

	North	
	♠ K 5 3 2 ♡ A 9 7 ◇ K ♣ A Q J 4 2	
West		East
♠ Q 10 8 ♡ K 8 ◇ Q J 10 6 3 ♣ K 9 7		♠ A J 9 ♡ 6 2 ◇ 9 8 7 4 2 ♣ 8 6 5
	South	
	♠ 7 6 4 ♡ Q J 10 5 4 3 ◇ A 5 ♣ 10 3	

"I held the South hand and became declarer, the contract being *four hearts*. The opening lead was the diamond queen.

* Willard Karn was considered to be one of the nation's finest players. In the 1930's, he was a member of the team known as "The Four Horsemen," which also included P. Hal Sims, David Burnstine, and Oswald Jacoby. Of the four, only Jacoby is still alive—and he is the nation's top-ranking player.

This deal was taken from *Willard Karn Bridge Service*, published by Ray Long and Richard R. Smith, Inc., 1933.

"1.) Before playing the dummy's only diamond, the king, on the opening lead, I considered my combined North-South holding. I had contracted for ten tricks. With the proper reentries, I was sure of four clubs—possibly five—and five hearts—possibly six. The additional trick, in each instance, depended on a successful finesse for the king. I also had two diamond tricks. Hence, my contract was not in jeopardy *provided West did not obtain the lead to play spades through dummy's king.*

"2.) My conclusion was that I certainly could make ten tricks, if I afforded myself the requisite protection.

"3.) The next point that I considered was the question of reentries. The only hope for South (myself) was trumps, since dummy, after following to the first lead, would be void in diamonds.

"4.) Should dummy or declarer lead to trick two?

"These considerations caused me to overtake dummy's king of diamonds with my ace. I then played the heart queen. West covered, I won with dummy's ace, and returned to my own hand with another trump. Next, I finessed clubs and was able to discard three losing spades on dummy's long clubs and use dummy's last trump to ruff my diamond five. I found that I had made all thirteen tricks.

"The thoughts outlined above passed through my mind within a minute, nor should they require abstruse calculations on the part of anyone at all accustomed to playing. Nevertheless, I found that practically everyone had played the same contract and had been favored by the same lead, but—for no authentic reason and merely *because the players did not stop to think through the entire situation*—dummy's king of diamonds was allowed to win the first trick in nearly every case! When this is done, it is impossible to exit from the dummy without losing a trick to West, either to his king of hearts or king of clubs. West, of course, then leads spades, and East-West will take three more tricks, thus setting the four-heart contract one trick.

"From this example, it is obvious that it is almost as dangerous, relatively speaking, for a declarer to plunge into play as it is for an automobile driver to hurtle over a crossing where the well-known 'Stop! Look! Listen!' legend is prominently displayed."

Deal 2:

The late David Bruce* (formerly Burnstine) was the South declarer. The deal arose in 1931.

"As a result of a bit of optimistic bidding, I became the declarer at a *six-club* contract on the following deal.

North
♠ J 10
♡ A Q 7
◇ A 8 4 3
♣ Q 8 4 2

West
♠ 9 8 5 4 3
♡ 9 5 2
◇ Q J 10 7 5
♣ —

East
♠ K 7 2
♡ 8 6 4 3
◇ K 6 2
♣ K J 9

South
♠ A Q 6
♡ K J 10
◇ 9
♣ A 10 7 6 5 3

"After West had opened the diamond queen, which I captured with dummy's ace, I was not happy with what I saw: a fifty-fifty loser in spades, and an almost certain trump loser. But this was not the time for regrets.

"I perceived that if the spade finesse lost, I would have to play the trump ace on the outside chance of catching the king. There-

* David Bruce, as the leading tournament player of the early 1930's, was accorded the honor of being made Life Master #1 when that category was inaugurated in 1936.

fore I promptly led the jack of spades and finessed. When it won, I heaved a sigh of relief. The spade loser had been eliminated.

"I could now afford to lose a trump trick, so I played it safe: I led the deuce of trumps, on which East followed with the nine. I inserted my ten—and West discarded the five of diamonds. My safety play had paid off! The ace of clubs next felled East's jack, and my only loser was a trump trick to East's king."

[I believe that many players would have gone down on this deal, for after winning the opening diamond lead, they would have led a trump to the ace—and East would now have had two trump tricks. But Burnstine foresaw that the normal tendency of drawing trumps immediately would have been wrong on this deal, for the key to the proper play in the trump suit depended on what happened in the spade suit: that if the spade finesse lost, he would be in dire straits, with success depending on avoiding the loss of a trump trick. But if the spade finesse won, then the avoidance of the loss of two trump tricks would become the order of the day. Hence his safety play of inserting the ten of trumps. Had West, in theory, won the trick with the jack, then the only trump outstanding would have been the king, which, of course, would be felled by declarer's ace when he regained the lead.—FLK]

Deal 3:

As a final illustration of the functioning of the expert minds of our primitive declarant ancestors, I would like to introduce the following deal, which arose in the Vanderbilt Cup Championships of 1935. The South declarer was Oswald Jacoby.

The bidding will probably not meet with the approval of the reader. By our current standards, expert bidding in the 1930's was chaotic and undisciplined. But, by dint of magnificent play, our forefathers managed to extricate themselves, and to attain the optimum result. This deal serves as a prime example of "bad bidding, excellent playing."

Neither side vulnerable. East dealer.

North

♠ A
♡ K J 7
◇ A 8 6 5 4
♣ A Q J 8

West	East
♠ J 8 3	♠ K Q 10 7 5 4
♡ A 10 4 2	♡ Q 9 6 5 3
◇ 7 3	◇ K
♣ 10 9 7 2	♣ 4

South

♠ 9 6 2
♡ 8
◇ Q J 10 9 2
♣ K 6 5 3

The bidding:

East	South	West	North
1 ♠	2 ◇	Pass	2 ♠
Pass	3 ◇	Pass	4 ♣
Pass	5 ♣	Pass	6 ◇
Pass	Pass	Pass	

West's three of spades opening lead was captured by dummy's ace. At trick two, Jacoby led dummy's king of hearts, West's ace winning. West returned a low club, Jacoby taking it with his king. The queen of diamonds was led next, and when West followed with the three-spot, Jacoby promptly put up dummy's ace, felling East's king. From here in the sailing was most pleasant, West's remaining trump being picked up and declarer's two losing spades being ruffed in dummy.

How many of our "modernists" would think of playing the king of hearts at trick two—before touching the trump suit—in order to find out which of the opponents held the heart ace? And then, upon perceiving that West was the possessor of that card, come to the conclusion that East just had to have the king of diamonds? And hence, the appreciation of the inevitability that if the diamond finesse were taken, it *had to lose,* for East, with neither the ace of hearts nor the king of diamonds, wouldn't have had the faintest semblance of an opening bid.

Thus, Jacoby created the condition that had to exist if his slam contract were to be fulfilled: East had to possess the singleton king of trumps. Jacoby then proceeded on the assumption that his creation was a reality—and it was.

chapter **2**

DECLARER'S PLAY: ARE EXPERTS "LUCKY"?*

I have been covering bridge tournaments for over three decades, for various newspapers and news services, and I've seen much good bridge and much bad bridge. The good bridge, unfortunately, does not get into print too often, since it usually takes a lot of space for proper presentation, and it invariably requires detailed analysis—not only of the actual play, but of the motives that were taken into consideration before selecting the winning line of play, as opposed to three or four alternative lines. As far as the newspapers are concerned, space limitation precludes such a lengthy presentation; and even if space were available, "good" play would be too complicated for the average bridgeplayer to digest at the breakfast table.

So what the newspapers and news services usually desire (and get) from the bridge reporter, as far as hands are concerned, is human-interest stuff: hands where an expert slipped, or hands on which an opponent got fresh against a name player and doubled him in some contract which the expert proceeded to fulfill with the assistance of either one or both of the defenders. Then the average bridge reader, still at the breakfast table, can turn to his wife and say: "And they call him an expert! If I were playing against opponents like that, I could have made the hand with my eyes closed!"

* The dictionary meaning of the word luck is: "that (fortunate thing) which happens to a person, *as if by chance,* in the course of events." I am using the word "lucky" in the above dictionary sense, as it is applied by bridgeplayers, i.e., a "lucky bridgeplayer" is one who receives gratuitous "gifts" (in the form of tricks) from naïve, gullible, and/or inept adversaries. The connotation is, of course, that the "luck" is undeserved, for it is not earned via merit.

Or—and this happens more frequently—after reading how the name player was the recipient of atrocious play by a couple of awe-stricken amateurs, the reader will turn to his better half and remark; "No wonder he wins so many tournaments! I could do the same thing if I got as many presents as he does. He sure is lucky!"

The above is, generally speaking, the newspaper presentation of bridge tournaments, and the hoped-for reaction by the reader. Admittedly, it makes good reading, but it is a distortion of the true situation. The expert is a human being and, as such, will slip on occasion. His errors and blunders, however, do not occur nearly as often as the newspaper "facts" would seem to indicate. And, as far as the newspaper approach that tends to give readers the impression that the expert is a very lucky guy who wins tournaments because Mr. and Mrs. Average Player hand him presents on a silver platter—nothing could be farther from the truth. Of course, in a national tournament event that is open to all players—for example, the National Open Pair Championship—the expert usually gets "lucky" breaks when playing against weaker opponents—but much more often than not he deliberately—and diabolically—creates the situations that are calculated to give him those breaks.

This chapter* is devoted to my attempting to refute what I consider the unfair designation of "lucky" which is so often used to characterize the winning expert player. I hope to accomplish my objective by introducing case histories of the expert in action, and thereby give the reader a glimpse into the functioning of the expert mind in the crucible of competitive play. If, after reading this chapter, the reader is still of the opinion that the expert is "lucky," the reader will be right—but I think he will agree with me when I say (and I do) that he deserves to be "lucky."

In each of the ten deals that comprise this chapter, the defenders had it in their power to defeat declarer, but didn't; or declarer, in fulfilling his contract, came up with a play that the average player would consider to be a "lucky" play. In each deal, declarer well deserved his victory.

* See also Chapter 5—"Defenders' Play: Are Experts 'Lucky'?"—which deals with "lucky" defenders.

Deal 1:

One of the attributes of the expert that enables him to extricate himself from apparently hopeless situations is the ability to capitalize on his knowledge of what the opponents are thinking; that is, to view a specific situation not only through his own eyes and mind, but also through the eyes and minds of his adversaries—as they are viewing it, as it were. For example, observe the following deal which came up in the National Championships of 1938.

Neither side vulnerable. North dealer.

North
♠ A K
♡ A Q 6 2
◊ A J 9 7
♣ A Q 8

West
♠ 10 8 6 3
♡ J 10 8 7 4
◊ 3 2
♣ J 10

East
♠ J 9
♡ 9 3
◊ K Q 10 8 5
♣ K 9 4 2

South
♠ Q 7 5 4 2
♡ K 5
◊ 6 4
♣ 7 6 5 3

The bidding:

North	East	South	West
2 ♡	Pass	2 NT	Pass
3 ◊	Double	3 ♠	Pass
3 NT	Pass	Pass	Pass

The reader will appreciate that the bidding is 1938 vintage—and I doubt seriously that the authorities of that day would have approved of North's "gay" bidding.

With East having doubled North's three-diamond bid, West made the normal lead of the diamond three, upon which the nine was played from dummy, and East captured the trick with his ten. East returned the king of diamonds, dummy's ace winning.

Declarer now paused for a few seconds, and then in rapid order came the ace of spades, the king of spades—and *the queen of clubs!*

Now, gentle reader, be honest. If you were sitting East, wouldn't you be certain that South possessed the jack of clubs, and that he was "sacrificing" dummy's queen to the king so that he could use the (presumed) jack of clubs as an entry to cash his established spades? And, having reached that conclusion, wouldn't you allow dummy's queen of clubs to win the trick?

Perhaps you would, and perhaps you wouldn't. In the actual play, however, East permitted the queen to win. Declarer now had his contracted-for nine tricks: three spades, three hearts, one diamond, and two clubs.

• • •

Deal 2:

One of the nation's top-ranking players is Meyer Schleifer of Los Angeles, California. Here is a picture of Meyer in action. The deal arose in a team-of-four event in Los Angeles in 1952.

The theme of this deal, by the way, is an unusual one. Normally, sound declarer's play when the opponents have bid is based on "an ear to the opponents' bidding." In this deal, however, Meyer came up with an unnatural line of play—the only winning line—because of *the failure* of an opponent to bid!

Both sides vulnerable. East dealer.

North
♠ A J 10 9
♡ 10 5 3
◊ 10 5
♣ 7 5 4 2

West
♠ 5 4 2
♡ 6 2
◊ Q 9 8
♣ K 10 9 8 3

East
♠ K
♡ A K Q J 9 8 4
◊ 7 3
♣ A Q J

South
♠ Q 8 7 6 3
♡ 7
◊ A K J 6 4 2
♣ 6

The bidding:

East	South	West	North
2 ♡	3 ◊	Pass	Pass
4 ♡	4 ♠	Pass	Pass
5 ♡	Pass	Pass	5 ♠
Pass	Pass	Double	Pass
Pass	Pass		

West opened the six of hearts, East's ace winning. The ace of clubs was cashed next, upon which West signaled vociferously for a continuation by playing the ten. The club queen was then played, South ruffing.

Meyer now led the three of spades, and when West followed with the deuce, dummy's ace was put up, dropping East's king. From here on the play was routine, declarer's diamond suit becoming established when West's queen fell on the third lead of the suit (dummy ruffing).

Why did Schleifer go up with dummy's trump ace instead of taking the finesse for the king? Here is the way he explained it to me:

"East had opened with a game-forcing two bid—he was known to have a powerhouse hand. Assuming that the opponents were not falsecarding, when East laid down the ace of clubs at trick two, West had signaled most encouragingly with the ten. To me, West surely had the club king, especially when East continued with the *queen* of clubs at trick three. *Had West also held the spade king—in back of my spade overcall at the four-level—he surely would have taken some action over my four-spade bid.*

"But West had passed, making it almost certain that East possessed the spade king, and that a spade finesse, if taken, was a cinch to lose. So my only hope was that East's spade king was a singleton. Luckily, it was."

The logic of Meyer's reasoning is easy to agree with in retrospect, but to come up with his play in actual competition is another matter. How many of us, I wonder, would have fulfilled our doubled five-spade contract?

• • •

Deal 3:

According to Webster, deception is defined as "the art of misleading." As applied at the bridge table, deception might be described as the attempt to get your adversary to think as you want him to think, to get him to believe that some unreality is actually a fact—in brief, to lead him on, and then have him discover belatedly that what he thought was reality was nothing more than a mirage.

It is perhaps unfortunate that the word "deception," as applied to real life, is associated exclusively with the social connotation of "fraud" and "deceit," and is considered not nice. And of course the deceiver is frowned upon by society. But in bridge, deception is considered to be a wonderful personality trait to possess, and its possessors are looked upon as the wise, the good—and the expert.

Here is an example of deception achieving the desired effect.

Neither side vulnerable. South dealer.

North
♠ Q J 10 9 4
♡ 5 3
◇ Q 7 5
♣ 9 4 2

West
♠ 6 5
♡ A Q 8 6 4
◇ 10 9
♣ J 8 6 3

East
♠ 8 7 3
♡ 10 7 2
◇ A J 6 2
♣ Q 10 5

South
♠ A K 2
♡ K J 9
◇ K 8 4 3
♣ A K 7

The bidding:

South	West	North	East
1 ◇	Pass	1 ♠	Pass
3 NT	Pass	Pass	Pass

West opened the six of hearts, and East's ten was captured by declarer's jack. It was obvious to declarer that West held the ace and queen of hearts, for if East had held either of these cards he would have played it on the opening lead. Declarer was also pretty sure that East held the diamond ace, for if West had held that card he probably would have overcalled the one diamond bid with a one-heart call (West was known to have a heart suit headed by the ace and queen). Declarer, of course, had just eight tricks: five spades, one heart, and two clubs. And when a diamond would be led by him eventually, East would put up his ace and return a heart, ambushing declarer's king, and enabling West to cash his entire heart suit.

But if East could be deceived into believing that dummy's spade suit was unreachable, then declarer could "steal" his ninth, and game-going trick. And so, at tricks two and three, declarer played his ace and king of spades—and stopped. He then plunked down the king of diamonds!

From East's point of view, he felt that if he took the king with the ace, dummy's diamond queen would become an entry for the cashing of the three high spades. So he allowed the king of diamonds to win. Declarer now scooted home with nine tricks.

Please don't criticize East. From his position, declarer might well have had the A K J of hearts, instead of the K J 9.

This deal arose in the National Mens Pair Championship of 1948. As it happened, North-South were experts—East and West were not. Had East and West been expert defenders, declarer would not have gotten away with his camouflage. At the upper echelons, when a declarer is trying to establish a long suit in dummy, a defender will give a "high-low" signal when he has an even number of cards in the to-be-established suit. In the above setup, on declarer's leads of the ace and king of spades, West would have played the six and five, respectively. Thus, East would have known that West had only two spades—and that declarer still had one left. Knowing this, East would, of course, have taken the diamond king with the ace, to return a heart.

• • •

Deal 4:

Way back in 1934, Richard L. Frey, paired with Howard Schenken, won the Masters Pairs Championship for the famous von Zedtwitz Gold Cup. Mr. Frey was at that time—and still is—one of our foremost players and analysts. Here is an example of his thinking in 1934. The narration is by Mr. Frey,* who was the South declarer.

Neither side vulnerable. South dealer.

North

♠ K 6 2
♡ K 10
◇ A 10 8 4 3
♣ J 9 7

West

♠ J 8 7 5
♡ A Q 4
◇ 6 2
♣ Q 5 3 2

East

♠ 9 3
♡ 7 5 3
◇ Q J 7 5
♣ A 8 6 4

South

♠ A Q 10 4
♡ J 9 8 6 2
◇ K 9
♣ K 10

The bidding:

South	West	North	East
1 ♡	Pass	2 ◇	Pass
2 NT	Pass	3 NT	Pass
Pass	Pass		

"By way of apology for the bidding, it must be explained that, as will happen in a long session, I, South, made a mistake in sorting my cards and tucked a small spade in with my clubs. With the hand as actually held the better opening bid is one spade, reserving the heart suit as a rebid and avoiding the inference of greater strength which partner would be justified in gathering from a reversal of suit

* From *The Bridge World*, September 1934.

ranks—i.e., one heart, any response, two spades. But, of course, with the error in sorting I bid one heart, North responded two diamonds, I bid an optimistic two notrump, and my partner of course bid three notrump.

"West, with practically an even choice of leads, selected a low spade, which I won with the ten; and now, pausing to take stock, I suddenly made the gratifying discovery that I held four spade tricks. A low heart was led, West ducked and dummy's king was put up (the correct play in order to unblock the suit). The ten of hearts was returned and overtaken with my jack, and West's queen won the trick. West now shifted to a low club, East played the ace —and now came a triple-cross false-card.

"Regardless of the position of the queen of clubs, I could hope to win only one club trick, but it made a difference whether I won it sooner or later. An immediate club return would surely defeat the contract, since I still had to knock out the heart ace to produce the ninth trick. However, even without winning a club trick, I could still make my three notrump if I won four spades, three hearts, and two diamonds. I therefore dropped my king of clubs on the ace—a play that could not possibly lose a trick since dummy's jack and nine furnished a sure stopper.

"Now East began to do the thinking I had hoped he would. The bidding told him that I could not have a singleton club, else I would have rebid hearts or shown another suit instead of bidding two notrump. It was obvious, then, that I was falsecarding, and since I had dropped the king, East figured that I probably held the K Q alone and was trying to discourage a shift to some other until I could knock out the other heart stopper which his partner must hold. West had discontinued the spades himself; therefore, East reasoned, the shift that I was trying to avoid was diamonds. So, almost certain that West held the diamond king, East led a low diamond. I clattered up with the king and played the nine of hearts, which West, perforce, won with the ace. Helpless now to defeat the contract, West, in desperation underled his queen of clubs, and when my ten won I spread the hand, four-odd having blossomed on a branch that looked blighted indeed.

"In conclusion, I might add that I was playing against a strong team; in fact, had East been less alert and imaginative, my plans might not have worked. There's no sense in trying to triple-cross a player who wouldn't even suspect you of trying a double-cross."

Deal 5:

The ability to put up a brave front when he is actually in dire straits is one of the trademarks of the expert's strength. The effect of this "false front" is that it frequently misleads his adversaries into believing he is on safe ground, and they fail to press their advantage. As a consequence, the advantage now swings to the expert, and he usually doesn't let the opportunity slip away. Here is a case in point. The deal arose in a tournament held in Chicago in 1934.

Neither side vulnerable. South dealer.

North

♠ A 9 6
♡ 7 2
♢ K J 7
♣ K 10 9 4 3

West

♠ J 7 5 4
♡ K 10 6 4
♢ Q 8
♣ A 8 5

East

♠ 10 2
♡ Q 9 8 5 3
♢ 5 3
♣ Q J 6 2

South

♠ K Q 8 3
♡ A J
♢ A 10 9 6 4 2
♣ 7

The bidding:

South	West	North	East
1 ♢	Double	Redouble	1 ♡
Pass	Pass	2 ♣	Pass
2 ♠	Pass	3 ♠	Pass
3 NT	Pass	Pass	Pass

West opened the four of hearts, East covered with the queen, and South captured the trick with the ace. Here was South's thinking as he planned the play (with no absolute certainty that he was right).

"West's takeout double indicated that he was prepared for partner to bid spades, hearts, or clubs, and he therefore figures to have support for each of these suits. So he should be short in diamonds, which makes East a favorite to have the diamond queen. I'm going to finesse East for Her Highness. . . .

"If my finesse should happen to lose, I'll be in bad shape, for the opponents will then have me at their mercy in the heart suit. And yet, if my finesse loses to West, he may go wrong: he knows I have the jack of hearts,* but he might think I have it guarded; if he thinks so, he might be reluctant to lay down his king of hearts, for fear that if he did, he would establish my jack. Well, I just hope that East has the diamond queen, so that neither West nor I will have any problems."

At trick two, South led a diamond to dummy's king, after which he returned the jack of diamonds and took the finesse. West, as is apparent, won this trick with his queen.

West now thought long and hard. He evidently found it difficult to believe that South would be taking a dangerous diamond finesse if the latter had just a singleton jack of hearts left. At trick four, West, in a desperate effort to deceive declarer, led a low club away from his ace.

Declarer was not to be fooled, however. He knew that he couldn't afford to play low from dummy, for East would win the trick and play back a heart. So declarer climbed up with the board's king. When it held, declarer was home safely, with an overtrick.

It is perhaps anticlimactic to state that South actually made eleven tricks, but the fact is that he did. After winning with the club king, declarer cashed his diamonds and West was pressed for discards: in order to guard the jack of spades, he was forced to throw away the club ace and the two low hearts, leaving the king blank.

Declarer now played the king of spades, carefully following with the nine-spot from dummy; then came a spade to the board's ace,

* If East had held this card, he would have played it instead of the queen.

East dropping the ten. Dummy's heart was played next, putting West into the lead. West was now compelled to lead away from his J 7 of spades into declarer's Q 8.

All of which proves that if you give an expert a hand, he is apt to also take a foot. One just can't trust an expert.

Deal 6:

The difference between rubber-bridge thinking and duplicate (match-point) thinking can be evidenced on the next deal. It was played in the Masters Pair Championship of 1934, and the South declarer was Sam Fry, Jr., of New York City.

East-West vulnerable. North dealer.

North

♠ K 5
♡ A Q 9
◇ A K 6 4 3
♣ 10 3 2

West

♠ A J 9 4 2
♡ 7 6
◇ 10 5 2
♣ 8 7 4

East

♠ 10 8 6
♡ J 8 5 3 2
◇ 9 7
♣ A 6 5

South

♠ Q 7 3
♡ K 10 4
◇ Q J 8
♣ K Q J 9

The bidding:

North	East	South	West
1 ◇	Pass	2 NT	Pass
3 NT	Pass	Pass	Pass

West opened the four of spades and dummy's king won the trick. At rubber bridge, Sam would have had no problem: he would have "cashed out" for nine tricks and his contract. But this was a duplicate game, and factors other than the mere fulfillment of the contract had to be taken into consideration.

First, every other North-South pair figured to get to game at notrump. If North were the declarer, East might lead a suit other than spades (such as hearts or clubs, in theory), in which case North would make a sure eleven tricks. Or, if West had the club ace, then eleven tricks would be in the bag, by simply leading clubs at trick two and establishing that suit. Of course, if *East* had the club ace, and put it up when a club would be led from dummy at trick two and returned a spade, then the North-South contract would figure to collapse. But it just couldn't be right to settle for three notrump—at best, an average score—without giving it a try for an overtrick or two.

So reasoned Mr. Fry. At trick two he led dummy's *ten* of clubs, East played the five, and Sam put up his king, which held the trick. It was now certain that East held the club ace, for there were very few West players in the world, then and now, who would have declined to win the king if they had held the ace, especially when the possibility existed that East possessed the queen of clubs. Having "stolen" the club trick, Sam did not try to press his luck, and settled for one overtrick.

Of course, if East had put up the club ace at trick two, to play back a spade, Sam would have gone down, in which case he would probably have consoled himself with: "nothing ventured, nothing gained."

• • •

Deal 7*:

"Beware of the opponent who deliberately invites an attack in a certain suit. His motives are no more altruistic than those of the military strategist who purposely unguards a section of his front, as West, in the hand below, had occasion to learn. The bidding goes:

South	West	North	East
1 ♡	Pass	2 ◇	Pass
3 NT	Pass	Pass	Pass

North

♠ 7
♡ 9 6
◇ K 8 7 5 4 3 2
♣ 9 5 3

West

♠ K J 8 4 2
♡ Q 7 5
◇ Q
♣ K 10 8 2

East

♠ Q 10 5
♡ K 8 3 2
◇ J 6
♣ J 7 6 4

South

♠ A 9 6 3
♡ A J 10 4
◇ A 10 9
♣ A Q

* From an article by Frank Walker entitled "The Surprise Attack in Bridge" in *The Bridge World*, September 1932.

"After the spade opening, South studies the twenty-six cards at his disposal. He is perceptive enough to discover that, even with the favorable 2–1 distribution in diamonds, he will be blocked in his own hand after taking two rounds with the ace and king.

" 'If I can only throw away my nine of diamonds,' he muses, 'my troubles are over.' The inspiration comes. He keeps the ace of spades until the third round, thus perceiving that West has no more than five. Then he craftily lays down the diamond ace, finds the distribution to his liking, and exits with his last spade. On the fifth round of spades he discards his nine of diamonds and claims the balance of the tricks.

"Even though the attack was deliberately invited, it would have been an extremely clever West who did not cash his last spade and then look around for new worlds to conquer."

[All I have to say is that North's bidding was a justified tribute to South's playing ability.—FLK]

• • •

Deal 8:

Two of the basic weapons in the expert's arsenal of weapons are imagination and nerve. Here is an illustration of their utilization.

Neither side vulnerable. South dealer.

North

♠ A J 10 8 4
♡ Q J 10
◇ 6 3
♣ K J 10

West

♠ 5 2
♡ 9 8 5 3
◇ A J 4
♣ 9 7 4 2

East

♠ 9 7 6
♡ 6 4 2
◇ Q 10 9 7
♣ 8 5 3

South

♠ K Q 3
♡ A K 7
◇ K 8 5 2
♣ A Q 6

The bidding:

South	West	North	East
1 ◇	Pass	1 ♠	Pass
3 NT	Pass	6 NT	Pass
Pass	Pass		

When this deal arose in the National Womens Pair Championship of 1956, virtually every North-South pair arrived at a six-notrump contract. Only two pairs fulfilled this contract. One of these received the opening lead of the diamond ace, after which declarer exposed her hand and said, simply, "The rest are mine."

At the other table where the small slam was fulfilled, the deuce of clubs was opened. Sitting South was one of the nation's top women players, Mrs. Sally Johnson of New York City. She did not like her position, for the success of the contract seemed to depend on the fifty-fifty chance that East possessed the diamond ace, in which case the diamond king would become declarer's twelfth trick.

It was perfectly obvious to her that sooner or later she would have to lead a diamond off dummy and hope that East had been dealt the ace. She didn't dillydally.

After winning the opening lead with dummy's ten of clubs, she promptly led dummy's six of diamonds, East played the seven, Sally put up her king—and West followed with the four-spot, allowing the king to win! Mission accomplished.

From West's viewpoint, South had bid diamonds and "figured" to have a suit headed by the K Q. By declining to take the ace, West thought she might mislead South into believing that East held the diamond ace. In this case, South would subsequently make another diamond lead off dummy, and West would win two tricks.

Of course, if Sally had made the diamond play later instead of earlier, West would have had a better idea of what was going on. In all probability, she would then have taken her ace, and Sally would have gone down, as the rest of the field did.

Assuming we were all playing against this West defender, I wonder how many of us would have fulfilled our slam contract?

• • •

Deal 9:

In duplicate bridge, the fulfillment of a lowly one-notrump contract (when everybody else failed to fulfill it) is worth more, in match points, than the fulfillment of a vulnerable grand-slam contract in notrump if everybody else also fulfilled the latter. The reason, of course, is obvious: in duplicate bridge, you score one point for each team whose score you beat, and a half-point for each team whose score you tie.

Here is a deal where a South player, Irving Kass of New York City, received a bushel of points for fulfilling a one-notrump contract. The deal arose in a 1948 tournament.

Neither side vulnerable. East dealer.

North
♠ Q 6 5 3
♡ A 9 6 5 3
♢ 10 6
♣ 10 9

West
♠ 9 4
♡ J 10 4
♢ K J 7 3
♣ A Q 8 5

East
♠ K 10 8 7
♡ K 2
♢ 9 8 5
♣ K 7 3 2

South
♠ A J 2
♡ Q 8 7
♢ A Q 4 2
♣ J 6 4

The bidding:

East	South	West	North
Pass	1 ♢	Pass	1 ♡
Pass	1 NT	Pass	Pass
Pass			

West opened the nine of spades, dummy played low, East put up the ten-spot, and Mr. Kass's jack won the trick.

At trick two, Mr. Kass came up with a nicely conceived deceptive play: he led a low club towards dummy's ten! The purpose of this play was to implant in the opponents' minds the thought that *he* was interested in developing the club suit; and, thereby, to dissuade *them* from leading clubs.

West played low to the club lead, and East's king captured the trick. East, having observed that his partner had opened the nine of spades from what was obviously a short suit, concluded that the reason why partner hadn't led his long suit was that partner's long suit was hearts, dummy's bid suit. So, at trick three, in an attempt to establish West's presumed heart suit, East banged down the king of hearts. Declarer permitted this card to win (if he took it, there would be no way of reaching dummy to cash the to-be-established heart suit).

When West's discouraging four of hearts appeared on East's lead of the king, East abandoned hearts, and shifted to a diamond. But it was belated, for declarer now had his seven tricks: two spades, four hearts, and the ace of diamonds.

Had East returned a club at trick three (or a diamond), the one-notrump contract would have been defeated. But, since South was interested in clubs—he had led them first—East wasn't. South's deception had accomplished its purpose.

• • •

Deal 10:

This next deal features as beautiful a false-card as I have ever seen made by a declarer. Its practical effect was that it led the East defender into making a discard that was calculated to mislead (or at least not help) declarer. But, unfortunately, the discard misled West at the same time, with dire consequences. The deal was played in the early 1930's.

Neither side vulnerable. South dealer.

North

♠ 9 6 5
♡ Q 9
◇ A Q 7 4
♣ Q 9 6 5

West	East
♠ A K 10 8 7	♠ Q 3
♡ 10 8	♡ J 5 3
◇ 8 6 5	◇ J 10 3 2
♣ J 4 2	♣ A 10 7 3

South

♠ J 4 2
♡ A K 7 6 4 2
◇ K 9
♣ K 8

The bidding:

South	West	North	East
1 ♡	1 ♠	2 ◇	Pass
2 ♡	Pass	3 ♡	Pass
4 ♡	Pass	Pass	Pass

West opened the king of spades and followed up by playing the ace, East dropping the queen on the second spade lead. On this trick, South, having the feeling that it might be advantageous for East to believe that South had but two spades, played the *jack* instead of the four-spot! Although the jack was a winner if it had been preserved, South knew that it would remain so for but a fleeting second, until West would lead a third spade and East would ruff.

West now led the high ten of spades, and East, being absolutely certain that South was going to trump the trick, mechanically tossed away the three of clubs, inducing declarer (*and* West) to believe that East had no interest in the club suit. Declarer, of course, followed suit in spades.

The discard of the club three turned out to be suicidal. West, naturally, concluded that it was futile to lead a club in view of East's "noninterest"; and, by a process of elimination, decided that the defenders' hope lay in the diamond king being in the East hand.

And so, at trick four, West played a diamond, East's ten falling to South's king. Declarer now led all of his trumps, and this was the position prior to the lead of the last trump:

North

♠ —
♡ —
♢ A Q 7
♣ Q

West	**East**
♠ —	♠ —
♡ —	♡ —
♢ 6	♢ J 3 2
♣ J 4 2	♣ A

South

♠ —
♡ 4
♢ 9
♣ K 8

When declarer now led the four of trumps, discarding the board's queen of clubs, East became the victim of a squeeze. If he discarded the club ace, declarer's king would become his game-going trick. And if, instead, he tossed away the two of diamonds, dummy's A Q 7 would capture the last three tricks.

It is rather obvious that if declarer had not falsecarded with the jack of spades at trick two, West's third spade lead would have been ruffed by East. The latter would then have cashed the ace of clubs, for the setting trick.

Part of the blame for the faulty defense must be charged to West. When his partner dropped the spade queen on the second spade lead, he knew that declarer still possessed a spade. Had West now led a low spade (instead of the high ten), East would have trumped, after which he would have cashed the club ace, for the setting trick.

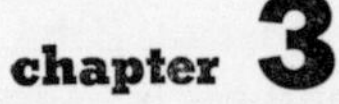

DECLARER'S PLAY: HOW NATIONAL CHAMPIONSHIPS ARE WON

In national championship events, where masters are pitted against masters, luck does not play a predominant role. At this top echelon, skill and psychology rise to the fore and are the elements that eventually determine the winners.

Within this chapter are presented nine deals culled from national championship play from 1930 to 1965. These deals illustrate the characteristics that produce winners:

1.) Table judgment (awareness of what is going on).
2.) An ear attuned to the opponents' bidding.
3.) Capitalizing on the knowledge of how an opponent is thinking.
4.) Technique, pure and simple.
5.) Creating an incorrect impression in a thinking opponent's mind.
6.) Why an opponent made a certain opening lead instead of another lead.
7.) A justifiable "underdog" play.

Deal 1:

The bridgeplayer who considers the psychology of his opponents—or of the specific situation—has an enormous advantage, whether the game be rubber bridge or tournament play. In rubber bridge, psychology is important only on swing hands, whereas at duplicate play no contract is too lowly to neglect the problem of obtaining the all-important extra trick.

The following deal arose in the National Championships held in Chicago in 1935. The South declarer, Miss Helen White,* came up with a play that was missed by all of the other experts who held the South hand. Her play was so psychologically sound, and so free from risk, that when pointed out it becomes simplicity itself.

East-West vulnerable. North dealer.

North

♠ A K 6 2
♡ 7 5
♢ 9 8 6 3
♣ A K 8

West

♠ J 9 7 4
♡ A Q 10 6
♢ Q 7 2
♣ J 6

East

♠ Q 8 3
♡ K J 9 8 4 3
♢ J 10 5
♣ 5

South

♠ 10 5
♡ 2
♢ A K 4
♣ Q 10 9 7 4 3 2

The bidding:

North	East	South	West
1 ♢	Pass	2 ♣	Pass
3 ♣	Pass	5 ♣	Pass
Pass	Pass		

* For those to whom the name "Miss Helen White" rings no bell, perhaps the name "Mrs. Helen Sobel" will. They are one and the same.

To even veteran duplicate players, an examination of the above deal will fail to reveal anything other than that the five-club contract is a routine one: a heart and a diamond have to be lost no matter what. But things aren't always as they appear to the naked eye.

West opened the four of spades, and the first thought in Helen's mind was that perhaps West was leading away from the Q J of spades. Admittedly, this was most unlikely (against a suit contract), but there was the theoretical possibility. . . .

Her thoughts then swung to East's play if the latter were permitted to win the first spade trick (assuming that Helen played low from dummy). North had opened the bidding with one diamond, and his four miserable diamonds lay exposed in dummy in all of their pitiful weakness. Barring a concentrated holding in hearts, East's normal shift at trick two would figure to be to diamonds.

So Helen played the deuce of spades off the board at trick one, and East won with the queen—and he did exactly as he was expected to do: he led the jack of diamonds.

South won with her ace, drew trumps with the king and queen, and then cashed her king of diamonds. She next led her remaining spade to dummy's king, after which she played the ace of spades, discarding her four of diamonds. A third lead of diamonds found each of the opponents following suit as Helen trumped. The dummy's fourth diamond had just been promoted into a winner.

The board was now reentered via the trump ace, and on the established diamond Helen discarded her losing heart. Thus she made a vital overtrick, for an undisputed top-score on the board.

• • •

Deal 2:

On the deal that follows, had South been playing in an average game, his well-calculated plan to create an incorrect impression in the mind of the West defender would have gone for nought.* But the deal happened to arise in the Masters Individual Championship of 1948, and each of the four participants was an acknowledged-by-his-peers bonafide expert. In this setting, South was able to pull off as neat a strategem as I have ever witnessed. Here it is:

Both sides vulnerable. East dealer.

North
♠ K J 10 4
♡ A 3
♢ J 7 5 2
♣ 7 6 4

West
♠ A 9 3
♡ Q J 9 7 4
♢ 6
♣ 9 8 5 2

East
♠ Q 8 7 6
♡ K 10 6 5 2
♢ 8 4
♣ 10 3

South
♠ 5 2
♡ 8
♢ A K Q 10 9 3
♣ A K Q J

The bidding:

East	South	West	North
Pass	2 ♢	Pass	3 ♢
Pass	4 NT	Pass	5 ♢
Pass	6 ♢	Pass	Pass
Pass			

* As the late Joe Penner was wont to say: "You can't fool me. I'm too ignorant."

After winning West's opening lead of the heart queen with dummy's ace, South perceived that his problem would be how to play the spade suit: when ultimately he would lead a spade from the South hand, and West would play low, should he insert dummy's king (hoping that West held the ace), or should he insert dummy's jack (hoping that West possessed the queen)? On his decision the outcome of the slam would rest.

South's first three leads were three rounds of trumps, one more than necessary. On the third trump lead, he discarded dummy's four of spades. Then came the ace, king, queen, and jack of clubs. On the latter trick, he tossed the board's remaining heart, the three-spot. He now led the five of spades.

Had West been a mechanical player, he undoubtedly would have followed suit with the three-spot, without undue haste or undue deliberation. South would then have had a pure guess as to what to play from dummy. But, happily for South, West had been watching closely, and had assembled these facts:

South was known to have started with exactly six diamonds, East having failed to follow suit to the third lead of diamonds. South was also known to have had precisely four clubs, since East had failed to follow to the third lead of that suit. When South had discarded dummy's remaining heart on the fourth club lead, it was "quite obvious" that South had a losing heart in his hand which he was going to trump with dummy's jack. Hence, since South had two hearts (he had followed suit to the opening lead of the heart queen), the five of spades which he was now leading had to be a singleton.

On this "logical" reasoning, West promptly put up the ace of spades, for otherwise he would lose it (so he thought). When it was all over, he realized, belatedly, that what he had thought was fact was only a mirage.

• • •

Deal 3*:

"The very first hand of the play-off for the Vanderbilt Cup brought about some interesting bidding and a problem in play.

"Mr. Sims, in the North, opened the bidding with a semi-psychic bid of one spade; Mr. Stearns, my partner, passed, and Mr. Karn, in the South, jumped the bidding to three spades. I, of course, bid four hearts. Here are the hands:

	North	
	♠ A J 10 9 8 ♡ Q 10 8 ◇ 10 6 5 ♣ J 3	
West		East
♠ — ♡ A J 9 7 6 5 4 3 ◇ A 4 ♣ A Q 7		♠ Q 6 4 2 ♡ 2 ◇ Q 8 2 ♣ K 10 8 5 2
	South	
	♠ K 7 5 3 ♡ K ◇ K J 9 7 3 ♣ 9 6 4	

"After two passes, Mr. Karn went to four spades. Being afraid to pass the bid to my partner for fear he would take no action (he would, of course, have doubled, for a two-trick penalty), I bid five hearts, which was passed all around.

"Mr. Sims led the ace of spades, which I ruffed. At this point I could tell that North did not have too much of a bid, as, after open-

* Taken from an article by Howard Schenken in *The Bridge World*, December 1931.

ing with one spade, he had let South do all of the subsequent bidding. I therefore led a small heart, hoping that South would get in, as I had him figured for the king of diamonds. After winning with the king of hearts, South led a low diamond and I decided to let it run to the queen, rather than take my ace and try for a discard on the long club suit in dummy. It developed that I had guessed correctly, as my queen won. North would have ruffed the third club had I played it the other way.

[By "had I played it the other way," Howard meant winning with the ace of diamonds, cashing the ace of trumps, and then playing the ace, queen, and a third club, hoping to discard his losing diamond on the fourth club in dummy. This line of play would succeed if North had three clubs—which he didn't.—FLK]

• • •

Deal 4*:

This is a deal from the Masters Pair Championship, 1930.

North-South vulnerable. East dealer.

Mrs. Ely Culbertson
North

♠ A 8 7
♡ A Q 10 9 8 7
◇ K
♣ A 10 5

Theodore Lightner
West

♠ K 2
♡ 4 3
◇ Q J 8 7 4
♣ 9 7 6 2

Mrs. P. Hal Sims
East

♠ 6
♡ J 5
◇ A 10 6 5 3 2
♣ Q J 4 3

Ely Culbertson
South

♠ Q J 10 9 5 4 3
♡ K 6 2
◇ 9
♣ K 8

The bidding:

East	South	West	North
Pass	1 ♠†	Pass	3 ♡
Pass	3 ♠‡	Pass	6 ♠
Pass	Pass	Pass	

* From an article by Ely Culbertson entitled "Between the Law of Symmetry and a Yawn," *The Bridge World*, August 1930.

"The whole play hinges on the question of the spade finesse. Mathematically with ten trumps the odds are so slightly in favor of a finesse as to be of itself a negligible factor. A more important factor lies in the *singleton* diamond king. I do not know by what mysterious channels of shuffle, but the fact remains that a singleton honor is frequently (too frequently) accompanied by a singleton honor in some other hand. I therefore decided not to finesse when —lo and behold!—I caught sight of a slight, partly-suppressed yawn in Teddy's mouth. Why should a man who is obviously wide-awake desire to yawn—unless a sudden excess of nervous energy seeks a physical outlet? And would he be so obviously excited if the king were not under the guillotine of the ace?

"On weighing the factor "Law of Symmetry" on one scale and the factor "slight twitching of the mouth muscle" on the other scale, I decided to finesse.* That board gave us a top."

• • •

---

† The proper bid is a pass. I chose that moment to make a "surprise attack" on Lightner, hoping to bluff him. . . . I was horrified to hear my partner (who naturally was also misled by my bid) tighten the noose of a slam bid around my neck with a forcing bid.

‡ To pass the forcing three-heart bid on the grounds that I held no opening bid might easily have cost us a game and result in a cold bottom. Besides, I *never* pass a forcing bid, not even in sleep.

* The half-camouflage bid and the play raise a question of ethics that might be confusing to many players. My camouflage bid was fair because in misleading the opponents I was at the same time running the grave risk of misleading my partner. As for profiting by mannerisms, it is perfectly fair to observe the *enemy* but it is equivalent to cheating to deliberately observe and profit by mannerisms, tone of voice, or gestures of one's partner.

Deal 5:

During the National Team-of-Four Championship of 1944, a hand arose about which it was written "the longest huddle in perhaps ten years must be credited to B. Jay Becker in his play. . . ." Here is that hand:

Both sides vulnerable. North dealer.

North

♠ A 9 8
♡ 9 8 4 2
◇ A K J 7 5
♣ A

West

♠ K 2
♡ K Q J
◇ Q 9 3
♣ J 9 7 3 2

East

♠ J 5
♡ A 10 6 5
◇ 10 8 2
♣ Q 10 6 4

South

♠ Q 10 7 6 4 3
♡ 7 3
◇ 6 4
♣ K 8 5

The bidding:

North	East	South	West
1 ◇	Pass	1 ♠	Pass
2 ♡	Pass	2 ♠	Pass
3 ♠	Pass	4 ♠	Pass
Pass	Pass		

West opened the king of hearts, then followed up with the queen. He next led the jack of hearts, which East overtook with the ace, Becker, South, trumping.

South's problem was to figure out the best way of drawing trumps to limit his loss therein to one trick; and, simultaneously, to save a trump in dummy for the ruffing of his losing club. Also, there was the consideration that if East won a trump trick while the opposition still possessed a few trumps, he would play the ten of hearts, thereby possibly giving his partner the opportunity of overruffing declarer.

If the spade suit were taken out of context, and one were asked how to play the suit in the best manner to restrict the loss to one trick, the answer would be to double-finesse. That is, lead a spade to the nine, and, upon regaining the lead, lead a spade to the eight. Whenever West has either the king or jack, five spade tricks will then be made. Had this been done, Becker would have gone down, since East, upon winning with the spade jack would have led the ten of hearts, and West would have made his king of spades via a ruff, for the setting trick.

Well, Becker thought and thought—and then thought some more. His partner, Mrs. Sobel, wandered around the room, read a magazine, and took a nap. His opponents gazed emptily at the ceiling, went out for a few drinks (of water), and chatted with the kibitzers.

After fifteen minutes (which is no exaggeration), Becker led a low spade to the ace, and a spade back. When the jack and king of spades fell on this trick, he spread his hand. The opponents spread theirs, revealing not only that the diamonds had broken 3–3, but that the finesse for the diamond queen was on if South wanted to take it (to get rid of his losing club).

"It must have been a tough hand," said Mrs. Sobel, returning to the table.

"No," said Becker. "It was a laydown."

• • •

Deal 6:

Alphonse Moyse, Jr., former editor of *The Bridge World* Magazine, is rather proud of his role in the following deal, which arose in the Vanderbilt Cup Championships of 1949. He was sitting South, and was partnered by Mrs. Kay Rhodes in the North seat. Sitting East and West, respectively, were Harry Fishbein and Lee Hazen, two of our nation's prominent internationalists. The narration is by Moyse.

North-South vulnerable. South dealer.

North

♠ K Q 9 2
♡ A K 10
♢ K 7 5 2
♣ A 6

West

♠ J 4 3
♡ 8 6
♢ J 6 4 3
♣ K J 7 5

East

♠ 6
♡ Q J 7 4 2
♢ 10 8
♣ Q 10 9 4 3

South

♠ A 10 8 7 5
♡ 9 5 3
♢ A Q 9
♣ 8 2

The bidding:

South	West	North	East
1 ♠	Pass	4 NT	Pass
5 ♡	Pass	5 NT	Pass
6 ♣	Pass	6 ♠	Pass
Pass	Pass		

"Hazen (West) opened a low trump. I won with the eight and drew two more rounds of trumps, ending in my own hand. Then, to give myself an extra chance, I tried the double heart finesse by leading a low heart from my own hand, and inserting dummy's ten. Fishbein took the ten with the jack and returned a heart. I collected dummy's ace and king and saw Hazen show out.

"I led a low diamond to my ace and took note of Fishbein's eight-spot. When I then cashed the diamond queen, the fall of the ten on my right gave me something to think about! In a case of this sort, I for one would really prefer not to get such a drop of the cards, because, with unimportant spots falling from Fishbein's hand, there would be only one possible play for the contract—to break the adverse diamonds 3–3. As it was, I had the sort of guess I don't relish! (Does anybody?)

"I laid down another trump and discarded dummy's club six, but, needless to say, that didn't bring me much information. Neither defender was apt to give up a diamond at this point. So I led the diamond nine, and when Hazen played the six, I went into a long huddle.

"There wasn't much to go by. Fishbein would have played the ten of diamonds on the second round from J 10 8 just as quickly as from 10–8 blank. Of course, there was the mathematical fact that a 4–2 break of the suit was more likely than a 3–3 break—but it was not that point which clinched my decision to let the nine ride. *It was Hazen's lead of a trump at trick one.*

"Hazen had possessed three spades headed by the jack and two worthless hearts. If he had three worthless diamonds, I felt that he would have tried a stab* lead rather than the passive trump lead. In other words, I thought that his only reason for selecting the trump lead was that he had *some* protection in *two* suits, not just in clubs. Such subtle factors exert quite a bit of influence over an expert's lead against a slam. (Afterward, Hazen admitted that he *had* been influenced by his possible stopper in both minor suits)."

• • •

* Aggressive.

Deal 7:

In 1964, Mary Jane Farell of California supplanted Helen Sobel as the nation's No. 1 woman player in the national rankings. The deal which follows depicts Mary Jane in action. The deal arose in the Life Masters Pairs Championship held in 1965.

East-West vulnerable. East dealer.

North

♠ 10 3
♡ A 10 8 5
◊ K 8 7 4
♣ 10 8 5

West	**East**
♠ J 9 8 6 5 4	♠ Q 7 2
♡ J 6 2	♡ Q 9 4 3
◊ 2	◊ A J 3
♣ J 9 7	♣ K 4 3

South

♠ A K
♡ K 7
◊ Q 10 9 6 5
♣ A Q 6 2

The bidding:

East	South	West	North
1 ♣	Double	1 ♠	2 ♡
Pass	3 NT	Pass	Pass
Pass			

West opened the seven of clubs and East's king was captured by Mary Jane's ace. A diamond to dummy's king brought out East's ace. East continued the club suit, declarer played low, and West won the trick with his jack. West returned a club, and South now had three club tricks.

Mary Jane now led a heart to dummy's ace, after which she played the diamond eight, letting it ride. When it won, she took the rest of the tricks, eleven in all.

What prompted Mary Jane to take that finesse for the diamond jack? As she put it: "East had made a vulnerable opening bid on a trash hand and a broken-down three-card club suit. West had shown up with the club jack and figured to have the spade jack for his bid. The percentage was that a vulnerable East had the jack of diamonds."

Yes, West could have had the jack of diamonds instead of the jack of hearts, but I like Mary Jane's percentage answer. East figured to have both red jacks, which would bring his hand to a thirteen-point total. I am certain that even the most ardent pro-male chauvinist—who is convinced that men are infinitely superior to women as bridgeplayers—would be willing to say that Mary Jane played the hand "like a man."

To concretize the above point, the deal was played twenty-six times, by twenty-five men and Mary Jane Farell. None of the other twenty-five South players made as much as three notrump with two overtricks.

Deal 8:

In the upper echelons of bridgedom, one of the subjects that is discussed quite often is the issue of whether defensive bidding (overcalls, takeout double, preemptive bids, etc.) is of greater practical assistance to the defenders than it is to the declarer. That is, does the bidding by the ultimate defenders guide the defenders to the winning line of defense more often than it guides declarer to the winning offensive line of play? In these discussions, the consensus of opinion is that usually, in the long run, the defenders show a greater profit through their "intrusions" (setting up their defenses) than does the declarer, who has been "listening in" to the clues that have been articulated.

Despite the above conclusion, it is an accepted fact that quite frequently the defenders' bidding illuminates the way to proper declarer's play, thereby enabling declarer to bring home a contract that might well have gone down had the defenders elected to remain quiet.

Here is a deal in which the bidding by each of the defenders literally told declarer how to play the trump suit. Sitting South was Margaret Wagar of Atlanta, Georgia, one of the finest players of all time. The deal arose in the National Open Pair Championship of 1947. Mrs. Wagar, partnered by Helen Sobel, won this blue-ribbon event; and the two of them repeated in 1948, only the second time in the forty-year history of this event that the same pair has won this event two years in a row.

North-South vulnerable. South dealer.

North
♠ J 9 7 5
♡ K J 10 3
◇ Q 7 4 2
♣ A

West
♠ 2
♡ A 8 6
◇ K 9 6 3
♣ K 8 6 5 2

East
♠ K 10 4
♡ 9 7 2
◇ A J 10
♣ 9 7 4 3

South
♠ A Q 8 6 3
♡ Q 5 4
◇ 8 5
♣ Q J 10

The bidding:

South	West	North	East
1 ♠	Double	Redouble	1 NT
Pass	Pass	4 ♠	Pass
Pass	Pass		

West's takeout double denoted the theoretical ability to play the hand at hearts, diamonds, or clubs—and hence indicated an extreme shortness in spades. East's notrump bid showed a stopper in spades, South's bid suit. When dummy came into view, it appeared quite reasonable to assume that East probably had three spades headed by the king. Mrs. Wagar proceeded to play the hand on this assumption.

Against the four-spade contract, West opened the five of clubs, dummy's ace winning. The jack of spades was then led, covered by East's king, and captured by South's ace. The queen of clubs was played next, on which West put up the king, and dummy ruffed with the nine of spades. The board's five of spades was then led, East followed with the four, and Mrs. Wagar inserted her six-spot, successfully finessing against East's ten. The ace of spades came next, felling East's king. Eventually South lost two diamonds and a heart, her only three losers.

Had the defenders not bid, Mrs. Wagar's first trump lead off dummy probably would have been a low spade, with the queen being finessed. This would have won the trick, of course, but East would still have had the K 10 remaining, and could not have been prevented from eventually winning a spade trick.

In the absence of any East-West bidding, the lead of a low spade off dummy would avoid the loss of a trump trick if East had been dealt a singleton or doubleton king; and would restrict the trump loss to just one trick if East had been dealt no spades, with West possessing the K 10 4 2. But, with the bidding having gone as it did, it was a virtual impossibility that East was either void of spades or the possessor of the singleton king; and, conversely, it was quite probable that East had either three or four spades, headed by the king. Hence the finesse not only against the guarded king, but also against the ten-spot, became the order of the day.

• • •

Deal 9:

One of bridge's classic deals arose in the Masters Team-of-Four Championship held in 1957. It illustrates the psychology that is often employed by a master team which considers itself to be an underdog in a match, and feels that it must on occasion resort to abnormal, anti-percentage play if success is to be attained.

North-South vulnerable. South dealer.

North

♠ K 7 3
♡ A J 10
♢ A K 10 3
♣ A K 2

West

♠ 9 6
♡ Q 9 5
♢ Q 9 8 7 4
♣ 6 5 4

East

♠ 5 4 2
♡ 7 4 3 2
♢ J 2
♣ 9 8 7 3

South

♠ A Q J 10 8
♡ K 8 6
♢ 6 5
♣ Q J 10

The bidding:

South	West	North	East
1 ♠	Pass	2 ♢	Pass
2 ♠	Pass	4 NT	Pass
5 ♢	Pass	5 NT	Pass
6 ♢	Pass	7 ♠	Pass
Pass	Pass		

Sitting South was Pedro Cabral of New York City, paired with Sally Johnson of New York, sitting North. They were part of a team playing against the international team of John R. Crawford, Sidney Silodor, Alvin Roth, Tobias Stone, George Rapee, and B. Jay Becker. At the end of the three-quarter mark, the Cabral team was 2160 points behind. This was the fifty-sixth, and final, deal.

Against Cabral's seven-spade contract, West opened the four of clubs, which was won by dummy's king. Three rounds of spades picked up the adverse trumps, after which declarer cashed the ace of diamonds, the king of diamonds, and then trumped a diamond. On this latter trick, East discarded a club.

Declarer next played the ace of clubs, and followed with a club to South's queen. He now paused to survey the situation.

By observation, East was known to have possessed three trumps, two diamonds, and four clubs (he had followed to three club leads, as had everybody, and had discarded a club on the third lead of diamonds). Hence, he had to have started with four hearts, while West had started with three hearts. Mathematically speaking Cabral knew that East figured to possess the queen of hearts. And, of course, the grand slam hinged on a successful heart finesse.

But Cabral also realized that his team was behind. And he figured that when the deal would be replayed, his most capable opponents at the other table would also arrive at a grand-slam contract (they did). Further, he knew that the other South declarer would also discover that East had four hearts and West but three; and that South would, as a percentage play, finesse East for the heart queen.

So Cabral, trying to create a "swing," deliberately took the anti-percentage play of finessing *West* for the heart queen. As luck would have it, the finesse worked, and he scored 2310 points (counting the one hundred honors).

When the deal was replayed, a grand-slam contract in notrump was arrived at by Cabral's opponents at the other table, Alvin Roth (South) and Tobias Stone (North). As Cabral had hoped for, and surmised, Roth finessed East for the heart queen, and went down two tricks when West also cashed the diamond queen.

Thus, the Cabral team gained 2510 points on this final deal, and won the match by the slender margin of 180 points.

DEFENDERS' PLAY

chapter 4

DEFENDERS' PLAY: PROLOGUE

As was stated in passing earlier in this text: ". . . of the three departments of bridge—bidding, declarer's play, and defenders' play—the most difficult to master is defenders' play. . . . Scientific development in the field of defense has lagged far behind the scientific development of bidding methods and techniques of declarer's play. There are relatively few guiding principles to point the way to proper defense. As a consequence, a defender is frequently on his own because the pattern of correct defense varies greatly from deal to deal. Many diverse defensive situations arise where there exists no precedent to take a defender by the hand and lead him to the desired objective. In these situations, judgment and/or imagination must operate independently of any established, governing law. . . ."

From the defenders' point of view, in order to attack and counterattack successfully, they must, of necessity, use as a springboard the few scientific principles that are available to them. These consist of a system of "conventional opening leads" and a system of "conventional signals." With the application of these principles of standard leads and standard signals, the defenders are able to convey to each other the proper line of defense. It is, of course, mandatory—for their self-preservation—that each partner by continuously on the alert to receive and correctly interpret whatever scientific information his partner is attempting to transmit.

By utilizing the above approach, the natural difficulties that are inherent in proper defensive play can be reduced, and guesswork areas can be narrowed. And, as a consequence, fewer defensive mistakes will be made, which, in a tournament, gives the keen defenders a tremendous edge over their competitors. It is, of course, an accepted fact of bridge living that victories are won not by being brilliant, but rather by making fewer mistakes than one's competitors.

It is not my intention, within this text, to discuss or illustrate the basic, time-honored, systems of conventional leads or signals. It is assumed that the reader is familiar with such things as "the lead of the fourth from the highest against notrump contracts," the "high-low signal" (come on, partner!), the "negative signal" of a low card (no interest in this suit, partner), etc. If the reader desires full coverage with respect to the subjects of standard leads and standard signals, he can obtain them in any of a half-dozen books on the play of the cards.

Within these chapters on defensive play, there will be presented situations wherein defender's primary guide was his spur-of-the-moment appraisal of how to best resolve successfully the problem at hand. The deal-by-deal illustrations, in describing the functioning of the experienced, brilliant, expert mind, will show how his imagination rose to the fore when necessity so demanded; how, when an immediate, unilateral decision became imperative, he was not afraid to make it; and how, when a defender could have played it safe and found refuge in a sanctuary that was offered gratuitously by orthodoxy ("conventional" leads and "conventional" signals), he chose to become unorthodox because he felt it was the correct position to take. In brief, the emphasis will be on digression and deviation from "normal" modes of accepted, dogmatic, defensive behavior. The aim of this approach is to inculcate in the reader an understanding of *why* the expert reasoned as he did, acted as he did—and triumphed as he did.

Lest the reader infer that I am deriding conventional leads and conventional signals, I would like to state most emphatically that I am not. As a matter of fact, many of the feats of defensive mental agility which will be presented could not possibly have developed unless conventional leads and signals served as the foothold. Thus, the reader can be assured that I am not minimizing the importance of the foundation that has been established over the past four decades. It is simply that I am taking it for granted and consciously ignoring it, while discussing the perhaps invisible heights to which the superstructure can soar through the application of the thought processes and imagination. Perhaps my position would be better understood if I said that I concur completely with the statement: "Man cannot live by bread alone."

As was done in Chapter 1, "Declarer's Play: Prologue," I would like to introduce three representative deals that confronted three of our "primitive" forefathers. The purpose is to give the reader a glimpse into the functioning of the expert mind. It will be observed from their imaginative defense in these deals that we have good reason to be very proud of our ancestry.

Deal 1:

In retrospect, West's two discards on the following deal would be approved of by all bridgeplayers as the only logical discards to make. Yet, at the table in real life, I doubt that one out of fifty of our nation's players would have made both of those discards—which happened to be the only ones that could have defeated South's game contract. Sitting West was the late Olive Peterson. The deal arose in a team-of-four match in 1936.

Neither side vulnerable. East dealer.

North
♠ 10 5 4
♡ K 9
♢ J
♣ K J 8 6 4 3 2

West
♠ 8
♡ J 10 5
♢ 10 9 8 6 5 4 2
♣ A Q

East
♠ A K Q 9 6 2
♡ 3
♢ 7 3
♣ 10 9 7 5

South
♠ J 7 3
♡ A Q 8 7 6 4 2
♢ A K Q
♣ —

East	South	West	North
1 ♠	4 ♡	Pass	Pass
Pass			

Mrs. Peterson's opening lead of the spade eight was taken by East's queen, after which East cashed the ace of spades, West discarding the club queen. East next led the spade king and Mrs. Peterson discarded—the ace of clubs!

East naturally shifted to a club, which declarer ruffed with the queen of hearts. Mrs. Peterson's heart jack had now been promoted into a winner, and it eventually took the setting trick. Of course, if declarer had trumped low on East's club return at trick four, West would have overtrumped.

From West's point of view, when East won the opening lead with the spade queen, it marked the ace and king of spades as being in the East hand. So Mrs. Peterson knew that she would be called upon to make two discards on the next two spade leads. The first discard of the queen of clubs didn't hurt a bit—with the exposed king of clubs in dummy, the queen was a useless card. When the king of spades was led at trick three, Mrs. Peterson fully appreciated that the ace of clubs would "almost surely" win a trick—if South had a club. But "almost surely" is not a certainty. If she tossed the ace of clubs, it would be perfectly obvious to East that she had no more clubs—and the then-guaranteed return of a club would create a trump winner for her. So she discarded the ace of clubs, and thereby made it an absolute certainty that the contract would be defeated.

• • •

Deal 2:

It is not very often that the word "brilliant" is used to describe an opening lead, but in my opinion that adjective is applicable to West's opening lead on this deal. The hand arose in a San Francisco tournament in 1943, and the West defender was the late Harry Merkle. I did not have the pleasure of ever meeting this gentleman, but according to some of our mutual friends, he was a truly great bridgeplayer.

East-West vulnerable. East dealer.

North

♠ 8 6 5
♡ K 9
◇ A 2
♣ Q 10 9 8 6 5

West

♠ A 9
♡ 10 8 4 3 2
◇ J 8 7 6 3
♣ A

East

♠ K Q J 10 7 3 2
♡ 6 5
◇ 9
♣ 7 4 2

South

♠ 4
♡ A Q J 7
◇ K Q 10 5 4
♣ K J 3

The bidding:

East	South	West	North
3 ♠	4 ♣	4 ♠	5 ♣
Pass	Pass	Pass	

South's four-club bid was the Fishbein Convention: a double by South would have been a penalty double, and a three-notrump overcall would have expressed the desire to play the hand at that contract. A bid of the next higher-ranking suit (in this case, four clubs) was for takeout.

As Mr. Merkle, sitting West, viewed the setup, it seemed to him that the best chance of defeating South's five-club contract lay in the hope that East had a singleton in either hearts or diamonds. If such were the situation, then if he could guess correctly which red suit to lead, upon regaining the lead with the trump ace he could return the original suit led, for partner to trump. But, obviously, it was a pure guess as to which red suit to lead. Nevertheless, Mr. Merkle had no trouble finding the winning lead.

Since East had made a vulnerable three-spade opening bid, it seemed to be almost a virtual certainty that he had the spade king. So Harry Merkle *led the spade nine at trick one,* underleading his ace! East rose to the occasion by overtaking the nine with his ten, and shifting to his singleton diamond, which was taken by dummy's ace.

A trump was then led, declarer's jack falling to West's ace. Mr. Merkle now followed through as planned—that East had a singleton in one of the red suits; and that suit had just become diamonds, based on East's lead at trick two—and returned a diamond, which East ruffed for the setting trick.

It was a *gorgeous* lead, was it not?

• • •

Deal 3:

Through the decades, Harry Fishbein has been famous not only because of his flawless technique, but also because of his imaginative declarer's play and defense. This deal depicts his imaginative defense. The hand came up in a Mixed Pair Championship event played in New York City in 1939.

North-South vulnerable. North dealer.

North

♠ 10 9 7
♡ 9 5 3 2
◇ Q 10
♣ Q J 10 4

West

♠ Q 4 3
♡ A 10
◇ A J 8 6 4
♣ 9 6 3

East

♠ 8 5 2
♡ Q J 7
◇ 5 3 2
♣ 8 7 5 2

South

♠ A K J 6
♡ K 8 6 4
◇ K 9 7
♣ A K

The bidding:

North	East	South	West
Pass	Pass	2 NT	Pass
3 NT	Pass	Pass	Pass

Fishbein, sitting West, opened the six of diamonds, dummy's ten-spot winning. Declarer now cashed the ace and king of clubs, after which he promptly led the jack of spades, offering it as bait. Had Fishbein taken the jack with his queen, dummy's ten of spades would then have served as an entry to dummy for the cashing of the queen and jack of clubs. But Fishbein declined the offering, and the jack of spades won the trick. When declarer next cashed the ace and king of spades—felling Fishbein's queen—he promoted his fourth spade into a winner. But all he could make were eight tricks: four spades, two diamonds, and two clubs.

When Fishbein was queried as to why he had defended as he did, he gave this explanation.

"Declarer gave the show away when he cashed the ace and king of clubs, and then cheerfully led the jack of spades. If he was so willing to give it away—presumably to make an entry out of dummy's ten of spades for the cashing of dummy's two high clubs—then it had to be wrong for me to take it. True, I figured to lose my queen by letting the jack win—but declarer figured to lose two tricks: dummy's clubs. So I gained a trick by declining declarer's offering.

"Incidentally, had declarer been a superior player, he would have made his contract. All he had to do at trick two—after winning my opening diamond lead with dummy's ten—was to lead a low spade and finesse his jack. At that stage, I would have had no reason to suspect what he was trying to accomplish, and I'm inclined to believe that I would have won the jack with my queen. I would then have cleared the diamond suit, with the hope that my ace of hearts would serve as an entry for the cashing of my established diamonds. But, happily, declarer gave me no opportunity to go wrong."

chapter 5

DEFENDERS' PLAY: ARE EXPERTS "LUCKY"?

In each of the eight deals that comprise this chapter, the declarer had it in his power to obtain the optimum result. He didn't—because he was outwitted by the defenders.

Deal 1:

Here is a swindle perpetrated by an East defender that is really a thing of beauty. It arose in a total point team-of-four event held in 1943, and the South declarer was one of the nation's top players.

East-West vulnerable. North dealer.

North

♠ A K J 9 2
♡ J 10 8 3
◇ K Q
♣ 8 4

South

♠ 6 4 3
♡ A Q 9 7 4 2
◇ J 9
♣ K 5

North	East	South	West
1 ♠	Pass	2 ♡	Pass
3 ♡	Pass	4 ♡	Pass
Pass	Pass		

West opened a low diamond, East's ace winning. After some thought, East returned the ten of spades, dummy's jack taking the trick as West followed with the five-spot.

Wouldn't you be just about absolutely certain that East had started with the singleton ten of spades? And that if the finesse in trumps lost (to a singleton king yet!) a spade would come back for East to ruff? Declarer sure was scared of that possibility.

So, instead of taking the trump finesse, he led a trump to his ace —after all, there was a decent chance of felling the singleton king. As it happened, however, both opponents followed suit with low trumps. A spade was now led, dummy's nine of spades being finessed successfully. Declarer's hope, of course, was to discard a club on the fourth lead of spades. But when he led the third round, East ruffed with the heart king and led back the queen of clubs. Two tricks later, declarer was down one. This was the actual setup:

	North	
	♠ A K J 9 2	
	♡ J 10 8 3	
	◇ K Q	
	♣ 8 4	
West		East
♠ Q 8 5		♠ 10 7
♡ 6		♡ K 5
◇ 10 6 4 3		◇ A 8 7 5 2
♣ A 9 7 3 2		♣ Q J 10 6
	South	
	♠ 6 4 3	
	♡ A Q 9 7 4 2	
	◇ J 9	
	♣ K 5	

From East's point of view, when he took the diamond ace at trick one, he indulged in the wishful thinking that his partner held the club ace. But even if this were true, it would not in itself be sufficient to defeat the contract, since it was obvious that the defenders couldn't make any tricks in either spades or diamonds. The hope, therefore, was that declarer could be talked out of taking the trump finesse, for fear that if it lost, dire consequences might result. And so out came the "singleton" ten of spades—and declarer fell for it, hook, line, and sinker.

Deal 2:

The psychological advantage possessed by the expert over the non-expert can be observed in the following deal which arose in a tournament in 1941.

Neither side vulnerable. South dealer.

North

♠ 6 5 2
♡ 9
◇ A K 10 4 2
♣ 10 7 6 3

West

♠ A Q 4
♡ K 10 7 3
◇ 9 7 3
♣ J 8 5

East

♠ K J 10 8 7
♡ Q 8 5 2
◇ 8 6 5
♣ 9

South

♠ 9 3
♡ A J 6 4
◇ Q J
♣ A K Q 4 2

The bidding:

South	West	North	East
1 ♣	Pass	1 ◇	Pass
1 ♡	Pass	2 ♣	Pass
3 ♣	Pass	4 ♣	Pass
5 ♣	Pass	Pass	Pass

West opened the ace of spades, receiving the encouraging ten-spot from his partner, and continued with the four, East's king winning. East came back with the spade seven.

Declarer, "knowing" that West had started with a doubleton spade, trumped the third spade lead with his queen. When he then cashed his ace and king of clubs, he discovered, to his sorrow, that West's jack of clubs had just become the setting trick. Had the four outstanding clubs been divided 2–2, declarer's ruffing of the third spade lead with the trump queen would not have been costly.

After it was over, declarer turned to our West expert and inquired: "How come you opened the ace of spades from A Q x? I was sure you had a doubleton."

The answer came out, simply: "Neither of you had ever bid notrump, so it must have been that you didn't have a spade stopper. My partner figured to have the king. Also, you had bid every other suit. Actually, I would have led a spade no matter what my spade holding had been."

Declarer's ruffing of the third spade lead with his queen was wrong for another reason: if West had started with the doubleton A x of spades, then East would have possessed the K Q J 10 x x of spades. Surely, with this holding, East would have bid some number of spades over North's one diamond response. But, as is obvious, declarer's reasoning did not go far enough—or, perhaps, he was afraid of the unknown.

• • •

Deal 3:

The National Open Team-of-Four Championship of 1942 was won by Peter Leventritt, Sam Rossant, Mrs. Helen Sobel, and Mrs. Margaret Wagar. Here is one of the deals that contributed to their victory, as narrated by Mr. Leventritt.*

Both sides vulnerable. North dealer.

North

♠ 9 7 6 5 4 3
♡ Q 10 6
♢ A Q
♣ A K

West

♠ Q 10
♡ J 8 5 3
♢ 9 7 5 2
♣ J 8 3

East

♠ J 2
♡ A K 9
♢ 10 8 6 4
♣ 10 6 5 2

South

♠ A K 8
♡ 7 4 2
♢ K J 3
♣ Q 9 7 4

The bidding:

North	East	South	West
1 ♠	Pass	2 ♡(!)	Pass
3 ♡	Pass	3 NT	Pass
Pass	Pass		

* From an article entitled "The National Tournament" in *The Bridge World*, January, 1942.

"I was sitting East, and Sam Rossant was West.

"South, of course, was trying to stave off a heart lead when he bid two hearts. My partner, however, became very suspicious at the course of the bidding, and defiantly opened the three of hearts. Dummy's ten was put in; I won with the king and led back the jack of spades. Declarer won and Rossant completed a brilliant performance by dropping the spade *queen.* Declarer "fell" with a bang! He entered dummy with a club, led back a spade, and when I played the deuce, finessed the eight-spot. Rossant produced the ten and then led another low heart.

"Now declarer was on the spot—was West trying to pull a fast one, underleading the ace, or did I have the ace? Anyway, he guessed wrong, put up dummy's queen and very soon found himself down one!

"Without intending to criticize my opponents, I must say that South's technique in this deal left something to be desired. His spade finesse was a magnificent example of an 'unsafety' play! The heart situation being what it was, he shouldn't have dared to let West get the lead. He could afford to give *me* a spade trick, if he had to; hence the plays of the ace and king of spades were mandatory as the best chance to keep West off the lead."

• • •

Deal 4*:

"A surprise attack of inspired conception was made by the West defender in a recent duplicate game. His reasoning was flawless and while the criticism might be advanced that such a hand comes up but once in the proverbial blue moon, when it does arise it spells the difference between victory and defeat.

Neither side vulnerable. South dealer.

North

♠ A K Q 9 5
♡ A K
◇ A Q 6
♣ 8 7 3

West

♠ 10 6 3
♡ 8 6 5 3
◇ J 8 3 2
♣ J 5

East

♠ 8 7 2
♡ Q J 9 7
◇ 10 9 7 5
♣ Q 2

South

♠ J 4
♡ 10 4 2
◇ K 4
♣ A K 10 9 6 4

The bidding:

South	West	North	East
1 ♣	Pass	2 ♠	Pass
3 ♣	Pass	3 ♠	Pass
3 NT	Pass	7 NT	Pass
Pass	Pass		

* Taken from an article by Frank Walker, "The Surprise Attack in Bridge," published in the September 1932 issue of *The Bridge World.*

"West decided that no normal opening lead would make a dent in the preponderance of honor tricks and distributional values held by his opponents. If South's club values were solid, the grand slam was probably a laydown. But, and the scheme began to formulate, if East held a club honor, the unimportant-looking knave in his own hand might attain some significance after all. Whereupon he led the five of clubs, East went up with the queen, and South won with the ace.

"Ensued five rounds of spades, two of hearts, and three of diamonds, and South found himself in dummy after the eleventh trick, with two clubs in dummy and the king and ten in his own hand.

"The opening lead had plainly placed East with the queen, knave, and deuce of clubs (when East followed with the deuce to trick twelve) and declarer finessed the ten with all confidence. West won with the knave and cashed a diamond, for a set of two.

"It is interesting to speculate what would have happened had East thrown away that vital deuce of clubs while in the throes of discarding. . . ."

[Had East thrown away the club deuce, West would undoubtedly have said to his *ex*-partner: "Oh, darn."—FLK]

• • •

Deal 5:

In this day and age, the deceptive false-card employed by West on the next deal would be considered old hat. But when the hand arose in 1932, the literature of that period described the play as "a magnificent false-card by the West defender. . . ."

Neither side vulnerable. North dealer.

North

♠ 6 2
♡ 10 8 5
◇ K Q J
♣ A K 9 6 2

West	**East**
♠ Q 10	♠ 8 5 3
♡ K Q J 6	♡ 9 7 2
◇ 9 7 5 3 2	◇ 10 8 4
♣ J 8	♣ Q 10 5 4

South

♠ A K J 9 7 4
♡ A 4 3
◇ A 6
♣ 7 3

The bidding:

North	East	South	West
1 ♣	Pass	2 ♠	Pass
3 ♣	Pass	3 ♠	Pass
4 ♠	Pass	6 ♠	Pass
Pass	Pass		

West opened the king of hearts, which was captured by declarer's ace. Declarer then laid down his ace of spades—and West followed with the *queen!*

Our declarer happened to be a good player, and he knew that the West defender was also a good player. Hence, from declarer's viewpoint, he knew that West might well have falsecarded from the Q 10 doubleton. But, then, the queen might have been a "true" play, that is, a singleton. Declarer, after some thought, decided that the queen was a singleton.

So declarer entered dummy via the jack of diamonds, and led the board's remaining spade, inserting his nine-spot when East followed with the five of spades. As is apparent, West won the trick with the ten and cashed two heart tricks, inflicting a two-trick set on declarer.

Had West played the ten of spades instead of the queen when declarer led the spade ace, declarer would also have had a problem as to whether to cash the king next or to finesse East for the queen.

Viewing it objectively, the fall of the queen on the ace would figure (in real life versus mathematical probability) to be a singleton more often than the fall of the ten would figure to be a singleton. After all, it does take nerve and imagination to toss the queen from the doubleton Q 10; and not too many players were capable of doing it in those days—or in these days, for that matter. And further, if the ten-spot were a singleton, then East would have started with the Q 8 5 3, in which case a spade trick would have to be lost even though a finesse for the queen would have been successful. Thus, I imagine that declarer would have laid down the king of spades next—if the ten had been played on the first lead—although the haunting thought would persist in his mind that perhaps West was falsecarding from the doubleton 10 5 or 10 8, trying to talk declarer out of finessing East for the queen.

At any rate, what would have been if West had played the ten instead of the queen on declarer's lead of the trump ace, we'll never know. But the result couldn't have been any more satisfactory to West than it was—and it could have been infinitely worse.

• • •

Deal 6:

The type of deceptive opening lead presented in this next deal has appeared in bridge columns literally scores of times since it first made its appearance in the National Men's Team-of-Four Championships of 1950. Here is the original rendition, as it occurred, with the actual participants.

Both sides vulnerable. South dealer.

North

♠ J 6 3
♡ 8 5
♢ A Q 7
♣ K 9 5 4 2

West	East
♠ 10 9 5	♠ K
♡ A 7 4	♡ J 10 9 3 2
♢ 9 5 4 2	♢ K 10 6
♣ A Q 6	♣ 10 8 7 3

South

♠ A Q 8 7 4 2
♡ K Q 6
♢ J 8 3
♣ J

The bidding:

South	West	North	East
1 ♠	Pass	2 ♣	Pass
2 ♠	Pass	3 ♠	Pass
4 ♠	Pass	Pass	Pass

Sitting South was John Gerber, of Houston, Texas. Gerber is famed not only for his invention of the Gerber Four Club Slam Convention, but also for his bridge prowess. In the West seat was Howard Schenken.

Against Gerber's four-spade contract, Schenken opened the *nine* of spades—and Gerber went into a deep study.

After the play of the deal had been completed, Gerber stated that he had been quite skeptical about a player of Schenken's stature leading a singleton trump . . . but on the bidding it was by no means impossible. So Gerber decided to believe the lead: it was either a singleton, or the top of a 9 5 doubleton; and East, therefore, held either the K 10 doubleton, or the K 10 5 tripleton. Up went dummy's jack of spades*—and Schenken's trump ten had just been promoted into a winner. With the subsequent loss of a club, a diamond, and a heart, Gerber's four-spade contract suffered a one-trick set.

Had a trump not been opened originally, Gerber would have breezed in with his contract. Left to his own resources, he would almost surely have led a low trump off dummy, intending to finesse the queen, and hoping that East had been dealt the doubleton king. If such were the distribution, then the loss of a trump trick would be avoided. Of course, on the low spade lead East would have had no choice but to play his singleton king, and declarer's ace, queen, and jack would have picked up all the adverse trumps.

But Schenken's "unnatural" lead of the spade nine resulted in declarer making an "unnatural" play—and provided bridge writers with a classic deal.

• • •

* In the actual play, it was Gerber's intention, after the ace of trumps took East's king, to reenter dummy and finesse East for the "marked" ten of spades (except, of course, if East showed up with the doubleton K 10, in which case the second finesse would become unnecessary).

Deal 7:

The deal that follows features a simple bit of deception by a defender who, as soon as dummy came into view, had formulated his plan. In recent years, with the passage of time, the type of play he came up with has become, in expert circles, a standard book-play. In the formative years of contract bridge, however—the deal arose in 1935—it was a spur-of-the-moment strategem.

Both sides vulnerable. East dealer.

North

♠ Q 7 5
♡ J 4 3
◇ 8 6 3
♣ K 5 3 2

West

♠ J 6
♡ 7 6 5
◇ 7 5 4 2
♣ 9 8 6 4

East

♠ A 9 4
♡ A 10 2
◇ K J 10 9
♣ A J 10

South

♠ K 10 8 3 2
♡ K Q 9 8
◇ A Q
♣ Q 7

The bidding:

East	South	West	North
1 ◇	Double	Pass	2 ♣
Pass	2 ♠	Pass	3 ♠
Pass	4 ♠	Pass	Pass
Pass			

West opened a diamond, his partner's bid suit, and East's nine was taken by declarer's queen. The deuce of trumps was then led to the board's queen—and East followed with the four-spot!

The five of spades was then returned, East covered with the nine, South put up his ten, and West's jack captured the trick. East subsequently cashed his three aces, sending declarer down to a one-trick defeat.

Had East taken dummy's trump queen at trick two, declarer surely would have made his contract, for in this case, being unable to reach dummy, he would have had no choice but to play his king of trumps, catching West's jack. East was fully aware of this position, for he perceived that dummy had no entries. By allowing dummy's queen of trumps to win, East accomplished two things: 1.) he led declarer to believe that *West* possessed the trump ace, and 2.) he enabled declarer to reach dummy to finesse East for the trump jack, if that card happened to be missing from declarer's hand.

Even if West happened to have the trump king (a virtual impossibility) East's play would cost nothing; or, if declarer happened to possess both the king and jack of trumps, then East would also be losing nothing by deferring the taking of his ace of trumps. But if declarer happened to be missing the trump jack, then perhaps he could be inveigled into finessing East for that card.

I'm glad that I wasn't sitting South on this deal. I hate to be tricked out of a nice game contract, especially when my partner has made a real fine bid in raising to three spades.

• • •

Deal 8:

One of the deals which aided the team of Mr. and Mrs. Charles J. Solomon of Philadelphia, Mrs. Sally Young of Bywood, Pennsylvania, and Peter Leventritt, of New York City, in winning the World Mixed Team-of-Four Championship of 1949, was the following:

East-West vulnerable. West dealer.

North

♠ A K 2
♡ 10 9 2
◇ A Q 8 6 5
♣ J 3

West

♠ —
♡ A K 5
◇ 10 7 3
♣ 10 9 8 7 5 4 2

East

♠ 10 7 6
♡ Q 8 4 3
◇ K J 9 2
♣ A 6

South

♠ Q J 9 8 5 4 3
♡ J 7 6
◇ 4
♣ K Q

With Mr. Solomon sitting East and Mrs. Solomon West, the bidding went:

West	North	East	South
Pass	1 ◇	Pass	1 ♠
Pass	2 ♠	Pass	4 ♠
Pass	Pass	Pass	

Against the four-spade contract, Mrs. Solomon opened the king of hearts, followed with the ace of hearts, and then played a third round of the suit, Mr. Solomon winning with his queen. After only a few seconds' hesitation, Solomon returned the six of trumps—and declarer looked like he had just received a reprieve!

From declarer's position, if the diamond finesse were successful, and the seven adverse diamonds were divided 4–3, then the contract would be fulfilled (the queen of clubs being discarded on the ace of diamonds, and the king of clubs on the fifth—soon-to-be-established—diamond). So South won East's trump lead with his queen, tried the diamond finesse—and went down two tricks.

Was Charles Solomon lucky? He sure was. But here's the way he reasoned it and forced declarer into an error. Declarer had shown up with exactly three hearts. Mr. Solomon had three trumps, and since there were three in dummy, declarer could have (at most) seven trumps. Therefore, declarer had to have at least three cards in the minor suits. From Mr. Solomon's seat, as he surveyed the field of combat, declarer just couldn't avoid the loss of another trick. Ergo, the trump lead, with the hope that declarer falls for it.

Technically, this next analysis does not belong in this chapter on "lucky" defenders. It is included, however, because it relates to the above deal. It illustrates what happened when the deal was replayed by Mr. Solomon's teammates, Sally Young, sitting North, and Peter Leventritt, South. The reader should find the replay quite interesting.

When Mr. Leventritt played the hand, the identical four-spade contract was arrived at via the identical bidding—and the play to the first four tricks was exactly the same, namely, three heart leads followed by a shift to the six of trumps. Mr. Leventritt won the fourth trick with the queen of trumps, after which the king and ace of trumps were cashed.

Now the jack of clubs was led off dummy—and East ducked! Mr. Leventritt captured the jack with his king, and then proceeded to lay down his remaining trumps, arriving at this position just prior to leading to trick eleven:

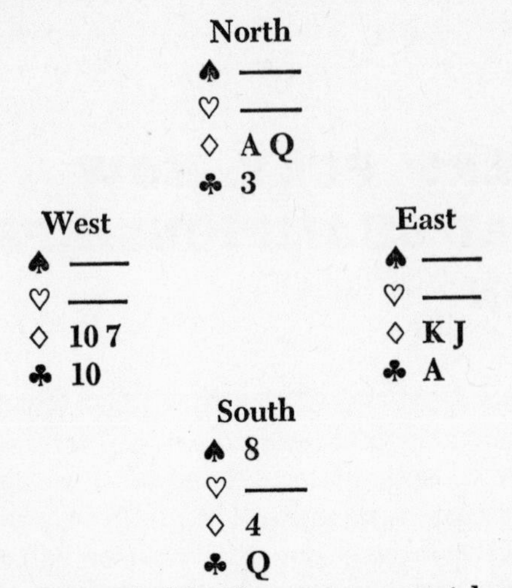

When Mr. Leventritt led his last trump at trick twelve, discarding the board's three of clubs, East was a dead duck. If he discarded the ace of clubs, South's queen would become a winner. And if, instead, he discarded the jack of diamonds, he would leave his king open to decapitation. East elected to discard the ace of clubs, hoping his partner held the queen—but to no avail. So Mr. Leventritt fulfilled an "impossible" contract.

Let me say that East's refusal to capture the jack of clubs (the setting trick) was a bad play. Nevertheless, East's naïve (shall we call it?) defense should not be permitted to detract from Mr. Leventritt's very neat play of the jack of clubs, which created the impression in East's mind that Leventritt was finessing for the queen.

When I spoke to Mr. Leventritt about the hand, he said that East just had to have the ace of clubs when he didn't lead clubs at trick four; and, furthermore, East also had to have the diamond king, for otherwise his trump lead would be "impossible." From East's viewpoint (as Mr. Leventritt viewed it), if he didn't possess the diamond king, then either South or West had it—and the "neutral" lead of a trump would automatically give declarer his contract.

And so the Solomon team really won this board—four spades bid and made at one table, and the same contract down two at the other table. Of course, "luck" entered into the picture, but, to use an analogy, in the same sense as "God is on the side of the heaviest artillery."

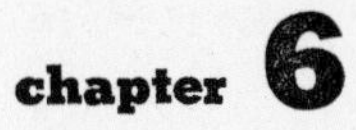

DEFENDERS' PLAY: HOW NATIONAL CHAMPIONSHIPS ARE WON

It has been pointed out that of the three departments of bridge—bidding, declarer's play, and defensive play—defensive play is the most difficult for all bridgeplayers to master, from the novice level through the most expert. In national championship play, those who are gifted with extraordinary defensive acumen will almost invariably emerge as the winners, for the defeating of the opponents' games and slams, and preventing them from making overtricks, pay handsome premiums in the form of match points.

Putting it another way, at the top level all experts are thoroughly proficient in bidding and declarer's play, the latter from the viewpoint of proper (mathematical) technique. This proficiency has been attained through years of study and practical application. But, on the other hand, in defensive play there has always been a dearth of knowledge, and new, previously unencountered situations are constantly arising for which there is no guiding precedent. Thus, a defensive expert who can correctly diagnose the situation confronting him, and respond properly, has a tremendous edge over his equally-expert adversaries who are not in his class, defensively speaking.

In this chapter are presented eight deals that arose in national championship play, in which the defense literally sparkled, and enabled the defenders to emerge victorious. The themes embodied are:

1.) Unorthodox opening leads, justifiably made.
2.) Forcing declarer to a guess.
3.) Prevention of an overtrick via a defensive signal.
4.) Imagination—the creation of a condition if defender were to avert a calamity.
5.) Sheer brilliance.

6.) Hope springs eternal.
7.) "A" for effort.
8.) An ear attuned to the opponents' bidding.

The deals were played in the years 1935 through 1950, inclusive.

Deal 1:

During the 1940's and 1950's one of the world's greatest players was John R. Crawford of Philadelphia. Here is an example of Crawford's skill in action. In this deal, which came up in the Vanderbilt Cup Championships of 1950, South was forced by Crawford to make a fifty-fifty guess. As it turned out, he guessed wrong, and it proved costly.

East-West vulnerable. South dealer.

North
♠ 6 3
♡ K 9 4
◇ J 10 7 2
♣ Q 9 5 2

West
♠ J 9 5 4 2
♡ 10 7 3
◇ A 8 3
♣ A 8

East
♠ A Q 7
♡ J 8 5 2
◇ Q 6 4
♣ J 7 6

South
♠ K 10 8
♡ A Q 6
◇ K 9 5
♣ K 10 4 3

The bidding:

South	West	North	East
1 ♣	Pass	1 ◇	Pass
1 NT	Pass	Pass	Pass

West opened the four of spades and Crawford, East, put up the queen, South's king winning.

A club was then led to dummy's queen, which held the trick, after which a low club was returned and declarer inserted his ten-spot, West being compelled to take the trick with his ace. West played back a spade, Crawford's ace winning.

At this point, most players would return their remaining spade, West would cash his three spades—and declarer would have his seven-trick contract wrapped up (three hearts, three clubs, and a spade).

But Crawford surmised that declarer had seven tricks all ready to take, and would take them if given the opportunity. So at trick five, after winning his spade ace, Crawford did not return his low spade —*instead he shifted to the four of diamonds,* thus putting declarer squarely to the test.

Our declarer was an excellent player—and, quite naturally, he knew that Crawford was an excellent player. Declarer fully appreciated that Crawford would just as surely have led a low diamond away from the ace as away from the queen. And Crawford knew that declarer knew this; and declarer knew that Crawford knew that declarer knew, etc., etc. The issue—the resolution of which couldn't be deferred—was: Is Crawford leading away from the ace or the queen?

After lengthy deliberation—with a look skyward for inspiration —declarer put up his king, playing Crawford for the diamond ace. It turned out to be the wrong guess, for the defenders were now able to take four spades, one club, and two diamonds.

• • •

Deal 2:

To a rubber-bridge player, the following deal would have no profound significance, for the only issue was whether declarer made an overtrick or two at his game contract. To a duplicate player, the issue would be—and was—a matter of life or death. The hand arose in the 1947 National Championships. Sitting West was Helen Sobel and East was Charles Goren.

Neither side vulnerable. South dealer.

North

♠ 10 5
♡ A Q 10 9 6 3
◇ A Q
♣ 10 9 5

West	East
♠ K Q 9 7 2	♠ 8 4 3
♡ K 5	♡ J 7 4
◇ K J 7	◇ 10 5 4 3 2
♣ Q 6 2	♣ J 8

South

♠ A J 6
♡ 8 2
◇ 9 8 6
♣ A K 7 4 3

The bidding:

South	West	North	East
1 ♣	1 ♠	3 ♡	Pass
3 NT	Pass	Pass	Pass

Mrs. Sobel chose to open the king of spades, rather than her fourth-highest spade. This lead, from the K Q 9, has a virtue at match-point play which is an important one: it is less likely to give declarer an overtrick than is the lead of the fourth-highest. On this deal it would not have mattered, but, as it turned out, with the king of spades lead, declarer happened to make a costly mistake.

South won the opening lead with his spade ace and laid down the ace of clubs (hoping to catch a singleton queen or jack, which would then enable him to make four club tricks). He then finessed the queen of hearts, successfully, after which he cashed the heart ace, felling West's king. A third round of hearts was next led, giving Goren his jack while simultaneously establishing dummy's heart suit.

On this trick, Mrs. Sobel made an excellent trick-saving discard: she tossed the deuce of spades, renouncing interest in the suit which she had opened at trick one.

Since it was perfectly obvious to Goren that Mrs. Sobel had no desire for him to lead back spades (except if he happened to possess the jack, in which case he would naturally cash that card), and since Mrs. Sobel could not possibly want a diamond lead, what with the dummy having the A Q, Goren laid down the jack of clubs, thereby establishing Mrs. Sobel's queen as a winner. Thus the defenders made a spade, a heart, and a club, holding declarer to ten tricks.

Had Goren returned a spade (upon winning the heart jack), declarer would have made a second spade trick, and, via a successful diamond finesse, a total of eleven tricks.

Had declarer not cashed his club ace at trick two, he would have made eleven tricks no matter what the defense did. But once he cashed that card, he gave the opponents an opportunity to develop a club winner.

• • •

Deal 3:

In the Masters Individual Championship of 1947, a beautiful bit of defensive thinking was turned in by the East defender, Bertram Lebhar. His imaginative defense gave him a top on the board, instead of a bottom.

Both sides vulnerable. North dealer.

North

♠ A K 8 3 2
♡ 8 3
◊ K J 9 5 4
♣ K

West

♠ J 10 6 5
♡ Q 10 7 2
◊ Q 3
♣ 9 5 2

East

♠ 9 4
♡ A K J 6 5
◊ A 10 8 7
♣ A J

South

♠ Q 7
♡ 9 4
◊ 6 2
♣ Q 10 8 7 6 4 3

The bidding:

North	East	South	West
1 ♠	Double	2 ♣	Pass
2 ◊	Pass	3 ♣	Pass
Pass	Double	Pass	Pass
Pass			

Lebhar's double of three clubs was of the "close" kind that is often made in a duplicate game when the opponents are vulnerable, the hope being for a one-trick set and a score of plus two hundred.

West opened a low heart, and Lebhar cashed his ace and king. He then paused to reflect about where the setting trick was coming from—*if* it were coming.

He found his sole hope. He led the ace of diamonds, and followed up with another diamond, North's king capturing West's queen. The king of clubs was then led, Lebhar's ace winning. A third diamond was now played—and there was no way for declarer to prevent West's club nine from taking the setting trick: if declarer trumped low, West would overtrump; and if declarer ruffed with his ten-spot, West would discard, and his nine of clubs would be promoted into a winner.

Lebhar was "lucky" in finding his partner with the 9 x x of clubs. Yet, how many of us would have capitalized on that luck?

• • •

Deal 4:

Back in 1947, the following report appeared in one of our nation's newspapers:

"Morrie Elis of New York City made a brilliant defensive play in the final round of the Vanderbilt Cup Championships. He was sitting East. Here is the deal and the bidding:

North-South vulnerable. East dealer.

North

♠ Q 10 3
♡ 8 5 4
◇ A 6
♣ Q J 10 5 3

West

♠ 8 6 5 4
♡ K
◇ K 10 9 8 4 2
♣ 9 4

East

♠ A
♡ A J 9 7 3 2
◇ J 5 3
♣ 8 6 2

South

♠ K J 9 7 2
♡ Q 10 6
◇ Q 7
♣ A K 7

The bidding:

East	South	West	North
1 ♡	1 ♠	Pass	2 ♠
Pass	2 NT	Pass	3 ♣
Pass	3 ♠	Pass	3 NT
Pass	Pass	Pass	

"West opened the king of hearts, which Elis overtook with his ace. Elis then shifted to the three of diamonds, upon which South played the queen and West covered with the king. Declarer permitted the king to win, but when West continued with another diamond, declarer had no choice but to win with dummy's ace. On this trick East unblocked by playing the diamond jack.

"All declarer could now make were eight tricks: five clubs, one diamond, and two hearts (the latter by finessing East for the jack of hearts). When declarer eventually led a spade, Elis took his ace and returned the five of diamonds, enabling West to cash his established diamond suit."

[Without a doubt, Elis' play was magnificent, and illustrated the heights to which the imagination of the expert can soar. But what motivated him to defend as he did? Here is his explanation.]

"When my partner opened the king of hearts, I knew it had to be a singleton. Declarer just had to have the Q 10 6 of hearts, for not only had he subsequently bid two notrump after I had opened the bidding with one heart, but he had done so voluntarily despite his partner's raise in spades. Assuredly, he had the heart suit protected.

"And so I knew that if my partner's singleton king of hearts were permitted to win the trick, he would have no choice but to shift to some other suit at trick two. As I viewed my hand and the dummy, whatever he shifted to figured to do us no good. Furthermore, I knew that no matter what I did, I could never establish and cash my heart suit.

"From my seat, the only chance we had to beat the contract lay in the diamond suit. So, with the wishful thinking that my partner possessed a diamond suit headed by the K 10, I overtook my partner's singleton king of hearts with my ace and shifted to a diamond. As luck would have it, the result was a gorgeous one. As to my tossing of the diamond jack on the second diamond lead, that was mandatory, for otherwise I could never get him into the lead to cash his diamonds."

• • •

Deal 5:

An ear to the opponents' bidding, *plus* the exercise of imagination, *plus* the hope that partner had an entry card, all combined to defeat declarer at his game contract in the following deal. The hand arose in a team-of-four match in 1935, and serves as an illuminating example of the functioning of the expert mind.

East-West vulnerable. South dealer.

North

♠ K 8 3
♡ A Q 7 6
◇ K 10 8 5 3
♣ 4

West

♠ 6 4
♡ J 3 2
◇ Q J 9
♣ J 9 8 3 2

East

♠ A Q J 5
♡ 10 9 8 4
◇ 6 4 2
♣ A 6

South

♠ 10 9 7 2
♡ K 5
◇ A 7
♣ K Q 10 7 5

The bidding:

South	West	North	East
1 ♣	Pass	1 ◇	Pass
1 ♠	Pass	2 ♡	Pass
2 NT	Pass	3 NT	Pass
Pass	Pass		

Against the three-notrump contract, West chose to lead a club (the three-spot) despite the fact that declarer had opened the bidding in that suit. East won this trick with his ace, and pondered over what to play back.

The club suit didn't appear to offer much hope: East had led, as his fourth-highest, the three-spot, which indicated that he had, at most, a five-card suit (which would be the case if he had the deuce, which he did). Hence, declarer possessed a minimum of five clubs.

This team-of-four match, incidentally, was a total-point game. In such a game, the defenders always exert a maximum effort to defeat a contract, even if by so doing they present declarer with an overtrick. Consequently, East's thinking was in terms of: "What's my best chance to beat three notrump?"

After some deliberation, East concluded that *if* West had an entry, the defense might triumph. At trick two, East led the five of spades!

South won this trick with his seven-spot, after which he laid down the ace of diamonds, and followed up with a low diamond, West's jack forcing dummy's king. A third lead of diamonds off dummy was captured by West's queen. The latter now dutifully returned his remaining spade, and East had himself three spade tricks. The third one was the setting trick.

It might have been (in theory) that when East switched to the spade five at trick two, he could be giving declarer an extra trick or two (which would have been the case if declarer had held, for example, the A Q of diamonds). But since the defenders' prime objective was to defeat the game contract, East's defense was proper—and the dividend was a handsome one.

• • •

Deal 6*:

During the past thirty years, the type of opening lead that was made on the following deal has been made frequently—but just about invariably in bridge columns rather than in real life. The student of the game, having read about this lead through the years, has appreciated its loveliness and has earmarked it for future employment. However, when the situation for its employment arises, the would-be-user turns coward, fearing either that the lead might cost him a trick, or that his partner may chastise him for becoming unorthodox all of a sudden.

But there are those who have the courage of their convictions; and if they have concluded that a lead is good in theory, they believe it is also good in practice. This deal involves one of those practical believers. It came up in a tournament held in 1937.

Neither side vulnerable. East dealer.

North

♠ Q
♡ 7
◇ A K 10 9 4
♣ K J 10 9 8 4

West

♠ K 6 4
♡ A Q 9 8
◇ 7 6 5
♣ A 5 2

East

♠ J 10 7 3 2
♡ 6 5 4 3
◇ J 3 2
♣ 3

South

♠ A 9 8 5
♡ K J 10 2
◇ Q 8
♣ Q 7 6

* The analysis of this deal is taken from Richard L. Frey's article, "Tops and Bottoms," *The Bridge World,* September 1937.

The bidding:

East	South	West	North
Pass	Pass	1 ♡	2 ◇
Pass	2 NT	Pass	3 ♣
Pass	3 NT	Pass	Pass
Pass			

It took West quite a while to decide what to lead. When he finally led, it was the *king* of spades that came out of his hand.

South permitted the king to win the trick, after which West continued with the spade six, East's ten being taken by declarer's ace. The queen of clubs was now led, West's ace winning. West returned his remaining spade, East capturing the trick with his jack.

From East's seat, it was virtually certain that West had no more spades (the lead of the king from K 9 x x would be going too far—but even if West held this combination, his second spade lead would not have been the six); and that, hence, South still had the spade suit protected with the nine spot. So East returned a heart, West's bid suit, and West cashed two heart tricks. Down one.

When queried as to "how come" he had opened the king of spades, West gave this answer:

"Although South had passed originally, when I bid one heart and his partner two diamonds, South went to two notrump. North's bid of three clubs, rather than three notrump, indicated that he had a two suiter, and that neither suit was particularly solid. South's rebid of three notrump, however, confirmed the fact that he held powerful heart stoppers, at least a trick in spades, and probably a fit with one or both of North's suits.

"Under these circumstances, a heart lead was out of the question and the lead of either diamonds or clubs would merely help the declarer to set up a lot of tricks. This left only the spade suit. I might have led a small spade, but I was anxious to put my partner in to lead hearts. Assuming that East had the spade queen, a low spade lead by me would have wasted that queen, leaving me with the high spade, and no reentry to my partner's hand. Finally, North's bidding indicated that he was short of both spades and hearts, and it was entirely possible that the spade king might drop a high spade honor from dummy."

Well put—and well done.

Deal 7:

Back in 1950 the first World Championship was held in Bermuda. Participating were three teams representing the United States, Great Britain, and Europe. The latter team, composed of four players from Sweden and two from Iceland, had earned the right to play in this event by having won a major team-of-four event held earlier that year in Europe.

The following deal was played in this World Championship, and serves as a good example of the functioning of the expert mind. Sitting North and South were Nils-Olaf Lilliehook and Jan Wohlin, both of Sweden. East and West were Joel Tarlo and Maurice Harrison-Gray, of Great Britain. The narration is by Alfred P. Sheinwold.*

"One of the neatest plays in the tournament was born to waste its fragrance on the Bermuda air.

East-West vulnerable. North dealer.

North

♠ 10 5
♡ 10 9 5
◇ K J 6
♣ A K J 10 4

West

♠ 4
♡ K J 6
◇ Q 10 8 7 4 3
♣ Q 5 2

East

♠ A 9 6 3
♡ 8 7 3
◇ A 9 5
♣ 9 8 7

South

♠ K Q J 8 7 2
♡ A Q 4 2
◇ 2
♣ 6 3

* From an article in *The Bridge World,* December 1950.

The bidding:

North	East	South	West
1 ♣	Pass	1 ♠	Pass
2 ♣	Pass	4 ♠	Pass
Pass	Pass		

"West opened a diamond, dummy played the jack, and East won with the ace. East returned the eight of hearts, South finessed the queen, and West won with the king. West shifted to the deuce of clubs, and dummy won with the king. The ten of spades was led next from dummy, holding the trick; and then East won the next spade lead.

"What should East return? East, Joel Tarlo, thought about this for a moment and came up with a very pretty answer—the nine of clubs, right up to dummy's strength!

"Tarlo could see that with any routine return (such as a heart or a spade), South would win and run all of his trumps. Eventually he would discover that West was squeezed to a pulp. If no squeeze worked, South could always take the club finesse (which Tarlo knew would be successful).

"With the club return, it looked as though Tarlo were now out of clubs. Should declarer discard one heart on the king of diamonds and then lead the ten of hearts for a finesse? That was the play Tarlo was trying to suggest to declarer.

"South, Jan Wohlin, looked long and carefully at the bait—and then ignored it. He cashed the king of diamonds and led a third high club from dummy, discarding his remaining losing heart. Tarlo had made a nice try, but it hadn't worked."

• • •

Deal 8:

The ability to break away from orthodoxy when the situation so demands is another of the characteristics that differentiates the expert from the run-of-the-mill player. Here is an example of this unorthodoxy in action, and the motivation that gave birth to it. The deal arose in a duplicate game in 1941.

Both sides vulnerable. North dealer.

North

♠ Q 10 7 5
♡ K Q J
◇ Q J 2
♣ A K 7

West

♠ K 3
♡ 10 7 6 5
◇ A 8 6
♣ Q J 10 2

East

♠ 8 6 2
♡ A 8 4 3
◇ 4 3
♣ 9 8 6 5

South

♠ A J 9 4
♡ 9 2
◇ K 10 9 7 5
♣ 4 3

The bidding:

North	East	South	West
1 NT	Pass	2 ◇*	Pass
2 NT	Pass	3 ♠	Pass
4 ♠	Pass	Pass	Pass

* Twenty-five years ago, any suit response to an opening notrump bid was considered to be a forcing bid.

Without any doubt, most bridgeplayers would have opened the queen of clubs against South's four-spade contract. Had this perfectly normal lead been made, declarer would have waltzed in with his contract, losing one heart, one spade, and one diamond.

But West, a very good player, had been listening closely to the bidding, to try to get some clues therefrom, and not merely to learn what the final contract was going to be. And he came up with what he thought sounded like a good piece of information.

Unquestionably South had five diamonds (perhaps even six), and North, who was known to have at least a doubleton diamond, might well have three of them. If such were the setup, then East was in a position to ruff the third lead of this suit (and, possibly, the second).

So, at trick one, West opened the ace of diamonds, and continued with the six-spot at trick two, dummy's jack winning. The queen of trumps was then led, and declarer took the finesse, losing to West's king. West now led a third diamond, East ruffing. East then cashed the ace of hearts, for the setting trick.

It could have been (in theory) that West's "ear-to-the-bidding" lead of the ace of diamonds, and the diamond continuation might not have gained anything, or, for that matter, might have lost a trick (which would have been the case had dummy possessed the ace of trumps, for West would then have been finessed out of his entry card, the king of trumps). Such losses have happened before, and will happen again. But, based on previously encountered similar bidding situations, West felt that the unorthodox lead was called for—and that it figured to gain more often than it figured to lose. Was that not sufficient justification for becoming a temporary iconoclast?

The Functioning of the Expert Mind: DECLARER'S AND DEFENDERS' PLAY

chapter 7

THE BRIDGE WORLD SPEAKS: 1929–1939

Although contract bridge was invented (by Harold S. Vanderbilt) in the year 1925, the recorded history of the game might be said to date from October 1929. The latter was the date on which the first issue of *The Bridge World* was published.

With respect to the game of bridge, *The Bridge World* has been our nation's sole recorder of the historical growth and development of contract bridge. It has registered not only the evolution of top-echelon bidding and play from birth, but has also concretized it with month-by-month illustrations of the expert mind in action as it progressed from infancy to maturity.

This chapter consists of the words of wisdom of some of the best players of the 1929–1939 era. Each of the deals presented depicts the unfolding of the thought processes of the expert as he sought for the solution to the problem confronting him.

Deal 1*:

This deal was sent to, and published in, *The Bridge World* by "an admirer of Harold S. Vanderbilt's," with the statement that "Mr. Vanderbilt played the hand as presented below, although he modestly failed to take credit for it."

* *The Bridge World,* October 1929.

Neither side vulnerable. North dealer.

North
♠ A K 8
♡ —
◇ A K 8 6
♣ A K J 10 8 2

West
♠ Q 9
♡ K J 10 6 2
◇ Q 7 5 3
♣ 7 5

East
♠ J 6 3
♡ 8
◇ J 10 9 4 2
♣ Q 9 6 4

South
♠ 10 7 5 4 2
♡ A Q 9 7 5 4 3
◇ —
♣ 3

The bidding:

North	East	South	West
1 ♣*	Pass	1 ◇*	Pass
2 NT	Pass	4 ♡	Pass
4 NT	Pass	5 ♠	Pass
6 ♠	Pass	Pass	Pass

"The play is most interesting and presents a number of unusual situations. West opens the diamond three. South then pauses to consider the situation and reasons as follows: 'Probably the slam will be attainable only if the adverse trumps are three and two;

* In the Vanderbilt Club System, then and now, an opening bid of one club was forcing. The one-diamond response was a negative bid, showing a poorish hand with respect to high cards.—FLK.

therefore such a distribution must be assumed at the outset. I cannot afford immediately to lead two rounds of trumps, otherwise I will have an insufficient number of entries in the dummy to establish the club suit. It is essential, of course, that the club suit be established and, for the last-named reason, this must be accomplished before the second trump lead. Therefore I must adopt every precaution to prevent a possible enemy club overruff in the short trump hand.'

"Accordingly, dummy wins the opening diamond lead on which South discards the club three. The two of clubs is then led and ruffed by South. At trick three, trumps are led, the dummy winning with the ace, and then the club eight is returned and ruffed by South, no club shortage having been observed in the opponents' hands. Trick five consists of a second round of trumps won by North with the king, both opponents following suit as West drops the queen.

"The winning adverse trump is now forced by leading the high clubs, and at the end of the hand South's trump and the heart ace are adequate to first ruff and then discard North's two losing diamonds, while North's remaining trump is used as a reentry for his remaining clubs.

"The slam is obtainable by no other than the correct method of play, as described above. The play of the hand is unusual because it involves:

1.) Discarding on the first trick an apparent card of entry into a hand when such cards are at a premium.

2.) Establishing a suit in the face of an adverse ruff before extracting the enemy trumps.

3.) A combination of the principles of husbanding of reentries; suit establishment by ruffing in the long trump hand facing an adverse ruff; adverse trump extraction; forcing of the good remaining adverse trump; and crossruffing all in one hand, and many of them in the inverse order to that in which they usually are accomplished."

[All in all, in current bridge parlance, a neat practical application of a "dummy-reversal" play. Incidentally, if East refuses to ruff either the fifth or sixth round of clubs, declarer discards a few of his hearts, after which he trumps a diamond, and on the ace of hearts discards dummy's fourth diamond.—FLK]

Deal 2*:

Partner's complete confidence is a player's greatest asset. The hand shown below, taken from a team match, well illustrates that fact.

Neither side vulnerable. South dealer.

North
♠ J 9 3
♡ 6 2
◇ Q 10 7
♣ K Q 10 8 7

West
♠ 8 7 2
♡ A K Q J 9
◇ K 9 6
♣ 4 2

East
♠ 4
♡ 10 7 3
◇ J 8 5 4 3 2
♣ A 5 3

South
♠ A K Q 10 6 5
♡ 8 5 4
◇ A
♣ J 9 6

The bidding went:

South	West	North	East
2 ♠	3 ♡	3 ♠	4 ♡
4 ♠	Double	Pass	Pass
Pass			

"Although the event dates back sometime, the brilliant work of

* From an article entitled "A Brilliant Defense," by E. V. Shepard, in *The Bridge World*, April 1930.

my partner is well worth relating. I was West and my partner was Mr. George Kling—one of our ablest players and most reliable partners.

"When I doubled, I knew that Mr. Kling would never let the double stand if he held more than four hearts or unless he held one of the missing minor aces. Evidently the declarer held six established spades and one side ace. Had more been held, South would have opened the contracting with a game declaration [bidding is circa 1929—FLK]. All this was clear as soon as I had led my heart king and viewed dummy.

"On its face, game should be made, and it would have been had I next led a second heart, but I did not want to part with control of my suit. We must make two heart tricks and my partner's minor suit ace, but we needed one added trick to defeat the contract: either I had to win a diamond or I must secure a ruff of a club.

"My lead of a diamond would be fatal in case declarer held the doubleton ace, as the lead coming up to him would rob me of my only possible trick in that suit. On the other hand, if my partner held that ace, I would lose in all probability by not leading diamonds.

"The numerous possibilities defied accurate analysis. I had to rely upon my ability to blindly pick the best minor suit to switch to. Instead of leading a second heart, I led my top club, trusting my partner to realize that I was leading a doubleton.

"The reliable one read my holding correctly: he gave me his best come-on, with his five, and we lost the trick. Now Mr. Declarer was in a fix—if he tried pulling trumps and found three in one hand, as my actions indicated, he could not ruff off his third heart, nor could he discard it on dummy's clubs, as I would ruff. He took two rounds of spades, and then led a heart. I won, and of course led my last club, secured my ruff, and put the contract down one trick.

"I only had to make a good guess at holdings, but my partner had the more difficult task of reading my holdings."

[It is apparent, of course, that if East had assumed that West was leading a singleton club, and the former won the first club lead to return a club, declarer would have made eleven tricks.—FLK]

• • •

Deal 3*:

Both sides vulnerable. South dealer.

North

♠ K J 9 7 3
♡ 5 2
◇ A Q 10
♣ J 7 4

West

♠ A Q 8 5
♡ A 8 6 3
◇ 6
♣ K Q 10 3

East

♠ 10 6 4 2
♡ —
◇ 8 7 5 4 3
♣ A 8 6 2

South

♠ —
♡ K Q J 10 9 7 4
◇ K J 9 2
♣ 9 5

The bidding:

South	West	North	East
4 ♡	Pass	Pass	Pass

"West led the king of clubs which, when it held the trick, placed the ace of the suit with East. West switched immediately to his singleton diamond which South won in dummy with his queen. West won the trump lead which followed with his ace, and led the

* From an article entitled "The Lead of a Singleton," by George Kling, published in *The Bridge World*, April 1930.

three of clubs, East winning with the ace and returning a small diamond which West trumped, saving the game, a beautiful defense."

[The above was the author's presentation of the facts. He then continued with the analysis, from West's viewpoint.—FLK]

"When his king of clubs held after the dummy went down, West saw at once that in order to save game, he must make two club tricks, the ace of spades, and the ace of hearts, or in lieu of the ace of spades, a second trump trick. Realizing that his trumps, outside of the ace, were utterly useless unless he could use them to ruff with, West led his singleton diamond as the best means of defeating the game. Having definitely placed East with the ace of clubs, because had South held the ace he would not have refused to win the king with three to the jack in dummy, West is absolutely assured of saving game if South has another club and East, when in with the second lead of clubs, will return a diamond.

"Only smart play will defeat this line of defense. At trick three declarer leads the king or jack of spades and discards his remaining club instead of leading trumps. This will prevent East from ever obtaining the lead and West never gets to trump a diamond."

[Re the final paragraph, the lead of the king of spades at trick three would have effectively broken East-West communication in clubs. However, if whichever of the opponents had the ace of hearts also had four diamonds, he would lead a third diamond, enabling his partner to ruff. (Assuming, of course, that whoever had the ace of spades returned a diamond at trick four.)—FLK]

• • •

Deal 4*:

"Someone recently remarked that the basis of sound play is card counting. Like all generalizations, this is but a partial truth. Personally, this writer inclines to the view that, in the long run, the faculty of drawing the logical inferences from the bidding, and incorporating them into a plan of play is more important. However, in the hand under discussion, the principle involved is simple and therefore a tactical review should be confined to fundamentals."

North-South vulnerable. South dealer.

North

♠ A K 9 5
♡ J 8
◊ J 8 6 5
♣ 9 7 3

West	East
♠ 7 4 3	♠ 10 8 6 2
♡ 9 7 3	♡ K Q 10 6
◊ Q 10 7 3	◊ 4
♣ K J 10	♣ 6 5 4 2

South

♠ Q J
♡ A 5 4 2
◊ A K 9 2
♣ A Q 8

The bidding:

South	West	North	East
1 ◊	Pass	1 ♠	Pass
3 NT	Pass	Pass	Pass

* From an article by Earl T. Robinson and E. C. Wolfe in *The Bridge World*, April 1931.

"Lacking a desirable lead, West opened the three of diamonds, and with the fall of the four of diamonds from East it is up to declarer—well, it is up to declarer to think.

"South can count as certain tricks four spades, one heart, three diamonds, and one club—a game, provided the ace and king of spades can be cashed without sacrificing one of his spade honors to enter the dummy. He must, of course, provide for the contingency that four spades inclusive of the ten may be bunched in one hand.

"From the opening lead of the three of diamonds, he knows that West holds four diamonds headed by the queen and that therefore he can never realize more than three tricks in this suit. The crucial play is thus that to the first trick South must play either the ace or king of diamonds to permit the knave of diamonds to serve as a sure entry.

"To the second and third tricks the queen and knave of spades are taken. To the fourth trick South cashes his other high diamond; and to the fifth trick he leads a low diamond towards dummy's jack, insuring game against any defense."

[The deal can serve as an object lesson for those who tend to win an opening lead as economically as possible, and then *belatedly* pause for reflection.—FLK]

Deal 5*:

"In preparation for the Eastern Tournament, it was decided to play a series of four match games between the halves of *The Bridge World* team, made up of Mrs. Culbertson and Mr. von Zedtwitz and Mr. Gottlieb and myself, Mr. Gottlieb taking Mr. Culbertson's place on the team.

"The play was very closely contested and resulted in a victory for Mr. Gottlieb and me by a very small margin.

"One of the more interesting hands was the following:

* From an article by Theodore A. Lightner entitled "Interesting Test Hands," *The Bridge World,* March 1932.

Both sides vulnerable. East dealer.

Mr. Gottlieb
North

♠ Q 2
♡ 10 9 7 5 4
◇ 7 4
♣ A J 7 5

Mrs. E. Culbertson
West

♠ 10
♡ K Q J 6 3
◇ 8
♣ K 10 6 4 3 2

Mr. von Zedtwitz
East

♠ J 8 7
♡ 8 2
◇ Q J 10 6 3 2
♣ Q 8

Mr. Lightner
South

♠ A K 9 6 5 4 3
♡ A
◇ A K 9 5
♣ 9

The bidding:

East	South	West	North
Pass	2 ♠	Pass	3 ♡
Pass	3 ♠	Pass	4 ♠
Pass	5 ♣*	Pass	6 ♣
Pass	6 ♠	Pass	Pass
Pass			

"In the play, Mrs. Culbertson opened the king of hearts, and Mr. von Zedtwitz played the eight to show his doubleton. I played two rounds of diamonds, the second being ruffed, much to my disappointment.

"Mrs. Culbertson, after long deliberation, played the queen of hearts. It is apparent that a club lead will defeat the hand, prevent-

* To confuse opponents and prevent a club lead.

ing the eventual squeeze play. Mrs. Culbertson, however, has a very hard guess, as on the bidding it looks as if I may have no clubs and will discard a heart loser on the ace.*

"After ruffing the heart queen, I took stock. I felt sure that Mrs. Culbertson had no more trumps or she would have returned a trump. Consequently, if I ruffed both of my losing diamonds, Mr. von Zedtwitz would have a spade trick—unless I could win the hand by a coup. On counting up, I found that I had too few entries in dummy for this play, so I considered a squeeze play, which could be seen to be a certainty at this point.

The final situation came out as follows:

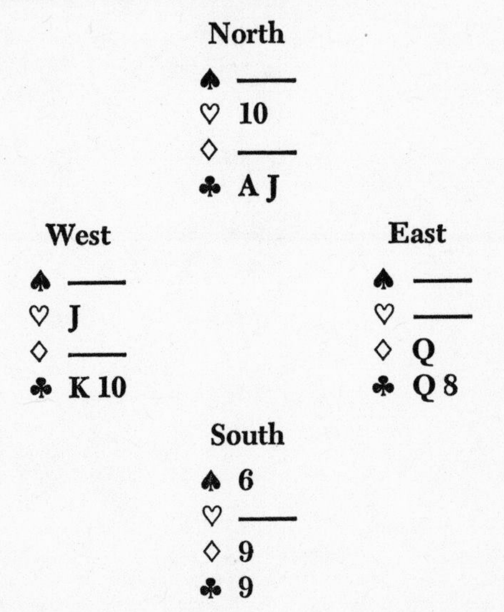

"On the lead of the last trump, West was forced to keep her heart knave, and so discarded the club ten. North discarded the ten of hearts, and East was compelled to keep the diamond queen. The king and queen of clubs then fell together on the next trick."

[After trumping the heart queen, Mr. Lightner ruffed a diamond with dummy's deuce, cashed the spade queen, ruffed another heart as Mr. von Zedtwitz discarded a diamond, and then cashed the ace and king of trumps, felling East's J 8. He then ran the rest of the trumps, and brought about the position presented in the above diagram.—FLK]

* The false cue-bid of "five clubs" paid a handsome dividend.

Deal 6*:

"In planning the play of a hand, it is often necessary to depart from the obvious and conventional methods when there is reason to suspect an unfavorable suit distribution. That good play and sound deduction is not confined to big-league players is shown by the manner in which the following deal was handled by Mrs. Bertha Maguire of Toronto, in a duplicate game at the Cavendish Club in Ottowa. [After observing Mrs. Maguire's play, I am sure that the reader will agree with me that she *was* a big leaguer, and probably playing under a pseudonym.—FLK].

Neither side vulnerable. South dealer.

H. B. Hatch
North

♠ A J 6
♡ K 10 8
♢ 7 6 3
♣ K 10 7 3

C. Sanger
West

♠ 7 3 2
♡ 6 4 2
♢ Q 10 8 5
♣ Q 9 2

Mrs. W. M. Anderson
East

♠ Q 10 9 8 4
♡ 9 5
♢ 9
♣ J 8 6 5 4

Mrs. B. Maguire
South

♠ K 5
♡ A Q J 7 3
♢ A K J 4 2
♣ A

South	West	North	East
2 ♡	Pass	3 ♡	Pass
4 ♢	Pass	5 ♡	Pass
6 ♡	Pass	Pass	Pass

* From an article by John W. Jacobson, entitled "The Safe Versus the Obvious Play," *The Bridge World,* June 1932.

"The two of hearts was opened, which was won by the king in dummy. Thirteen tricks were sure if the diamond finesse held or the queen dropped on the second round; the small slam was apparently assured.

"But why had West led a trump, Mrs. Maguire asked herself? Perhaps he had four diamonds to the queen. Mrs. Maguire therefore led a small diamond from dummy which was won with the ace in her own hand. She then entered dummy with a spade and led another diamond. Sure enough, East trumped, and the rest was easy.* Most players would have drawn two rounds of trumps and incurred sure defeat on an apparently unbeatable hand."

[If two rounds of trumps are drawn immediately, then when West obtains the lead with the queen of diamonds, he simply returns his remaining heart, removing dummy's last trump. In this case, West eventually obtains another diamond trick.—FLK]

Deal 7:

Captain Ewart Kempson, who passed away in 1966, was one of England's leading bridge authorities for over three decades. Back in 1933, Captain Kempson was a member of the British team that played a challenge match against the United States team headed by Ely Culbertson. In *The Bridge World* Captain Kempson narrated the story of one of the deals in that match. Here it is, verbatim.†

"When Ely Culbertson had finished with the thirty-fourth hand in his match against Captain Lindsay Mundy, I made a mental note of headlines for a bridge article.

"I dismissed 'Brilliant Defense by Ewart Kempson' as being a shade on the egotistical side, and substituted 'Ely at His Very Worst.'

* After cashing one more round of trumps, declarer simply led her king of diamonds, after which she trumped a fourth round of that suit.

† From an article entitled "When Ely Overrated His Opposition," *The Bridge-World*, September 1933.

East-West vulnerable. South dealer.

T. Lightner
North

♠ 9
♡ 4 3
◇ K 9 3 2
♣ A K Q J 7 2

L. Mundy
West

♠ J 8 6 3
♡ 9 8 7
◇ A Q 10
♣ 10 5 3

E. Kempson
East

♠ 5 2
♡ K Q J 5 2
◇ 6 4
♣ 9 8 6 4

E. Culbertson
South

♠ A K Q 10 7 4
♡ A 10 6
◇ J 8 7 5
♣ ——

The bidding:

South	West	North	East
3 ♠	Pass	4 ♣	Pass
4 ♠	Pass	Pass	Pass

"Captain Mundy led the nine of hearts, and East's knave was permitted to hold the trick.

"The normal lead from East's hand is a trump, as it is obvious from South's refusal to take the first trick that he holds at least one more losing heart. East, however, conceived the fantastic idea that a diamond offered the best chance of defeating the contract, so at trick two the six of diamonds was led. Captain Mundy won and returned the queen of diamonds, and dummy was in the lead.

"To the neophyte, the rest is easy: the ace of clubs provides a discard for West's losing heart, and the spades are played out, the knave being conceded to West.

"What actually happened was that, after discarding the offensive heart, Ely led dummy's spade and finessed the ten. West won, and the return of a diamond defeated the contract.

"Mr. Culbertson's defeat stamps him as a genius; his play was perfect, but, on this occasion, his judgment was lacking. For some reason, possibly because I told him that I was a magnificent player, he decided that I could not be such a gink as to lead a diamond unless I held five spades to the knave. Working on this assumption, he took the only possible chance of making his contract; he overrated my ability, and paid the penalty. . . ."

Deal 8:

During the 1930's, one of Canada's foremost players and analysts was John W. Jacobson, of Toronto. In the early years of the publication of *The Bridge World*, Mr. Jacobson was the editor of a column called "Bridge in Canada." Here is one of his columns taken verbatim from *The Bridge World.** If a title for this particular column were needed, I would suggest: "The Functioning of The Expert Mind: Fools Rush In . . ." Since virtually nobody is familiar with the writings of Mr. Jacobson, may I enlighten them by pointing out that he can be caustic and sarcastic while simultaneously maintaining a keen sense of humor.

"A number of my unappreciative readers have taken a cynical attitude toward the many brilliant bids and plays that I have described in this department for their enlightenment and edification. Those that I am in the habit of playing with regularly remark on the fact that the outstanding coups, defensive plays, etc., are invariably made by me, and the errors and miscalculations by my opponents, whereas, they unkindly remark, the exact reverse appears to be the case in actual play, especially when I happen to be their partner. Fearful of the effect this attitude may have on the circulation of *The Bridge World,* I feel it my duty to sit East and West from now on and allow my critics to occupy the South position, from which all the fine plays are made.

* "The Author Makes a Mistake," *The Bridge World,* October 1933.

East-West vulnerable. North dealer.

L. M. Wood
North

♠ A J 7
♡ K Q 4
◇ 8
♣ Q J 9 8 7 3

L. Maloney
West

♠ 6 4 3
♡ 5 2
◇ K 9 7 6 3 2
♣ 6 4

J. Jacobson
East

♠ Q 10 5
♡ A J 9 6
◇ A J 5
♣ A K 10

W. P. Slyne
South

♠ K 9 8 2
♡ 10 8 7 3
◇ Q 10 4
♣ 5 2

The bidding:

North	East	South	West
1 ♣	Double	Pass	1 ◇
Pass	1 ♡	Pass	2 ◇
Pass	3 NT	Pass	Pass
Pass			

"South opened a club, which I won, and led the ace of diamonds, followed by the knave, intending to give up this diamond trick in the hope of making five diamonds, three clubs, and a heart. But on the diamond knave, Mr. Slyne, ignoring all the rules covering fourchette positions, played the ten! What would you do? North was plainly marked with the lone queen, so I put up the king and made a total of six tricks. . . . Mr. Maloney inquired why I didn't play the hand the same way in real life as I do in *The Bridge World.*"

Deal 9:

The following deal, and the accompanying analysis, are taken verbatim from *The Bridge World.**

"Among his colleagues in Jersey City, Dr. Julius Siegler is known as a sound partner and a brilliant dummy player. His technique as declarer is well attested by his play of the following hand.

Neither side vulnerable. North dealer.

North

♠ 10 9 6 3
♡ A 7
◇ A K 7 5 4 3
♣ 7

West

♠ K 7 2
♡ J 10 9 6 4
◇ Q J 10
♣ 8 6

East

♠ Q 5 4
♡ Q 8 5 3
◇ 9 6
♣ A 10 9 5

South

♠ A J 8
♡ K 2
◇ 8 2
♣ K Q J 4 3 2

The bidding:

North	East	South	West
1 ◇	Pass	2 ♣	Pass
2 ◇	Pass	3 NT	Pass
Pass	Pass		

* From an article entitled "Doctors of Bridge," by the late Albert H. Morehead, in *The Bridge World,* January 1937.

"West opened the jack of hearts and Dr. Siegler, sitting South, studied the possibilities of the two hands. With only two heart stoppers, he could not afford to give the opponents the lead more than once.

"He could not afford to develop spades since the suit could not bring in more than three tricks and he could then run only seven tricks before giving the opponents the lead with a diamond or club to run the rest of their established hearts. And to set up the diamonds immediately would be no better since the opponents would then knock out his other heart and he would then run only five diamonds, two hearts, and one spade before he would have to give them the lead with the ace of clubs.

"By the process of elimination, Dr. Siegler arrived at the correct play. He won the opening lead with dummy's ace of hearts and led a club from the dummy. The writer, sitting East, dared not go up with the ace, for then South would have made the remaining five clubs for his contract and an overtrick.

"Having won the second trick with the king of clubs, South did not make the mistake of continuing the suit. At this point, it was safer to play for a 3–2 split of the diamonds than for a 3–3 split of the clubs. He therefore led one of his low diamonds and allowed West to hold the trick with his ten. Hearts were continued and Dr. Siegler won with his king and ran the diamonds and the ace of spades to fulfill his three-notrump contract.

[It might have been that West, rather than East, possessed the club ace. Had this been the case, a heart would have been returned, establishing the defenders' suit. Declarer would now have available, as a last resort, the 36 percent chance that the six adversely held clubs were divided 3–3. And a 36 percent chance is better than no chance, which would have been declarer's position if he attacked diamonds at trick two.—FLK]

• • •

Deal 10:

The deal which follows is related by the then-editor of *The Bridge World,* Alphonse Moyse, Jr.* It arose in the National Championship held in Cleveland in 1938. Mr. Moyse tells a sad, sad, story.

"This hand is reported with bowed head and blushes that would have done credit to the Victorian Era. I had to go all the way to Cleveland to get fixed as few players are fixed during a bridge lifetime! This little, luscious fruit came up in the first round of the Open Pairs.

Both sides vulnerable. South dealer.

North

♠ Q 8 6 3 2
♡ 10 5
◇ J 7 5
♣ Q 10 6

West	East
♠ J 10	♠ 9 5
♡ K 6 4 2	♡ J 9 3
◇ A Q 8 6	◇ K 9 4 3
♣ A J 3	♣ K 9 8 2

South

♠ A K 7 4
♡ A Q 8 7
◇ 10 2
♣ 7 5 4

The bidding:

South	West	North	East
1 ♠	Double	2 ♠	Pass
Pass	Pass		

* *The Bridge World,* January 1939.

"I was South—and lived to regret it! Not that the contract wasn't all right; it was the opening lead and continuation that sent me scurrying around Cleveland for sackcloth and ashes.

"Without a second's hesitation, the lady on my left laid down the ace of clubs and when her partner played the eight-spot, followed up with the three of clubs. Don't think that I made the second play from dummy in any carefree, blithe spirit! The huddle I went into must have set a record for longevity if not for productiveness. I even stole a side glance at the lady's face, but saw nothing but a cherubic expression. Said I to myself: 'Holy smoke, what's going on here? Is it possible that this gal is trying to give me the works with the old army play of laying down the ace from A K x, then following up with a low card to make me guess wrong? She certainly doesn't *look* that diabolical, but, then, who can tell about these women? It certainly seems more probable that she's doing that than that she would have laid down the ace from any holding of A J. Well, there's this much to be said for it: if I put up the ten and it loses to East's jack, and a club comes back to the king in the West hand, I'll have to go and cut my throat. On the other hand, if I put up the queen and it loses and a club comes back to the jack, I'll only have to hide for a few days. Because what a ribbing I'd take for falling for the very hoax play that I've written up so many times! Why, the boys would ride me out of Cleveland on a rail. Here goes!'

"The rest is history. I called for the queen, saw it smothered by East's king, and felt myself turning a deep magenta when East sent back a low club and West calmly, imperturbably (as though this were the most natural thing in the world) gathered in the trick with her jack.

"Naturally, I still had to lose two diamonds and a heart and therefore found that I had earned the dubious distinction of being the only South player among twenty-odd tables who had failed to make two spades. That was *one* of the boards that cost us the tournament."

chapter 8

"THERE, BUT FOR THE GRACE OF GOD, GO I"

Back in the sixteenth century, John Bradford, upon seeing prisoners taken to their place of execution, would exclaim: "But for the grace of God, there goes John Bradford!" This expression is now universalized, the implication being that under other circumstances, anyone might have fitted into another's place.

Within this chapter are presented eight deals which arose in top-level competition. The victims, in each case, could properly attribute their defeat to circumstances beyond their control. In each case, I am glad that I was not in the victim's seat at that time, for, if I had been, ". . . there . . . go I."

Deal 1:

You are sitting South, and have arrived at a *three-notrump* contract. There has been no adverse bidding:

North
♠ A 10 9 5
♡ A K
◇ Q J 8 7
♣ 9 8 4

South
♠ J 3
♡ Q 10 9 5
◇ A K 4
♣ Q 10 7 2

West opens the seven of spades, you play low from dummy, and East wins the trick with the queen. He then returns a heart which is taken by North's ace.

As you view the combined holdings—through your expert eyes—you perceive eight top tricks. You decide to go after the club suit for your ninth trick, with a chance of making two club tricks, which would be the case if East possesses the club jack.

At trick three, therefore, you lead the nine of clubs, East follows with the three-spot, and you play the deuce. To your great surprise, the nine wins the trick as West plays the five. The one thing that is now certain is that East possesses the jack of clubs. You next lead the eight of clubs—and East discards a spade! This was the setup:

North

♠ A 10 9 5
♡ A K
◇ Q J 8 7
♣ 9 8 4

West

♠ 7 6 2
♡ 8 4 3
◇ 9 6
♣ A K J 6 5

East

♠ K Q 8 4
♡ J 7 6 2
◇ 10 5 3 2
♣ 3

South

♠ J 3
♡ Q 10 9 5
◇ A K 4
♣ Q 10 7 2

East now proceeds to cash four club tricks—and you fold up your tent and silently steal away.

The deal arose in 1935, and the West defender was Pierre Albarran, the leading figure in French bridge until his death in 1960. And the South declarer was . . . one of our nation's top-ranking players, who, on this deal, I'm sure would prefer to remain anonymous.

Deal 2:

As can be observed from the preceding deal, when one plays against experts what appears to be reality on occasion turns out to be a mirage.

Here is another deal of the same general type as the preceding one. You are sitting South and, as an expert, you are paying close attention to what is being played.

North

♠ 7 5 3
♡ A 8 7 6
◇ 10 7 2
♣ K 10 5

South

♠ A K Q J
♡ K Q 3
◇ J 9 6
♣ A 8 4

Somehow or other, you have arrived at a *four-spade* contract, West having bid diamonds enroute. West cashes the three top diamonds, East discarding the deuce of clubs on the third diamond lead, after which West shifts to the *deuce* of hearts.

You, of course, play low from dummy as East puts up the ten, which you capture with your king. You next lead four rounds of trumps, West discarding his two long diamonds on the last two trump leads. Then you lay down the queen of hearts, West following with the four-spot as East drops the jack.

Surely, you say to yourself, West started with four hearts to the nine-spot (at trick four he had shifted to the deuce of hearts), and East started with the J 10 doubleton. So you lead your remaining three of hearts, and when West covers with the five you naturally insert dummy's eight-spot. You have just become a sadder, but, I trust, a wiser man.

Here are the four hands:

North

♠ 7 5 3
♡ A 8 7 6
◇ 10 7 2
♣ K 10 5

West

♠ 9 6
♡ 5 4 2
◇ A K Q 5 3
♣ J 9 6

East

♠ 10 8 4 2
♡ J 10 9
◇ 8 4
♣ Q 7 3 2

South

♠ A K Q J
♡ K Q 3
◇ J 9 6
♣ A 8 4

How about that! You thought that East's lead of the two of hearts was his fourth-highest? And was this thought not confirmed by East's plays of the ten and jack of hearts? How could you possibly have known that East, the dirty so and so, possessed the nine of hearts?

Well, you couldn't, I couldn't—and our actual declarer, a top-ranking Life Master, couldn't either. Even as you and I, he inserted dummy's eight of hearts, and East's nine-spot took the setting trick.

Deal 3:

The deal which follows was played in the National Open Pair Championship of 1951. Sitting East was Charles J. Solomon, currently the president of the World Bridge Federation, and one of our nation's top-ranking players for over three decades. In the West seat was Alphonse (Sonny) Moyse, Jr., the then-editor of *The Bridge World* magazine. The narration and analysis of the deal is by Mr. Moyse.

Both sides vulnerable. South dealer.

North
♠ 8 6 4
♡ A K 8
◇ K J 9
♣ J 7 6 2

West	East
♠ A Q 5	♠ 10 9 7 3 2
♡ Q 10 7 3	♡ 6 2
◇ Q 10 6 4	◇ 7 5 3
♣ Q 3	♣ 9 8 5

South
♠ K J
♡ J 9 5 4
◇ A 8 2
♣ A K 10 4

The bidding:

South	West	North	East
1 NT	Pass	3 NT	Pass
Pass	Pass		

"Listening to this bidding and looking at my own hand, it didn't need genius to conclude that partner Charlie must be busted higher than a kite. Well, I have a theory on such hands. I don't try to 'set up something' on the opening lead; all I want to do is not make things easy for declarer. So I didn't like a heart or a diamond opening—and why guess between them anyway? I laid down the ace of spades.

"Discussing the hand later, I found that several Wests had opened the queen of spades, but I'm sure that the ace is better. It isn't as though the prime objective were to make a miraculous find of five or six spades to the jack in partner's hand—I'll freely confess that that was only a faint hope. As already indicated, my main objective was to avoid the loss of a trick—and surely the ace serves this end better than the queen. If you lead the queen, you have a *very* good chance to lose it (without gaining anything); but if you lead the ace and, on sight of dummy, shift, you still have the queen back of the possible king in the South hand; and you may even have talked declarer out of a spade finesse if the king turns up in the North hand. I think readers will agree that, as between the ace and the queen, the choice isn't even close. In any case, the ace gives you a look at dummy.

"Of course with South holding the blank K J, it didn't matter which honor was led. Charlie gave me a hot come-on with the ten, and I followed with the queen, unblocking. But a lot of good it did me. South, in with the spade king, laid down the club king, then crossed to the board with a heart and led the club jack through East. Well, maybe there was a gleam in my eye, or maybe South was just too smart; whatever it was, the fact remains that he banged down his club ace—and broke my heart.

"On the next two club leads I was vindictive enough to discard the ten of diamonds, along with a heart, so that declarer *could* take the diamond finesse the wrong way if he felt like it, but I might have saved myself the trouble—this South was going to make his three-notrump contract, come hell or high water! Finesses, right or wrong, didn't interest him; he grabbed nine cold tricks.

"Please don't point out that I didn't have to beat my breast so hard, considering that South could have made a trick or two more. Mine was an artistic bitterness. And when I heard later that about half the East-West pairs had beaten three notrump with ease because *North* had played the hand and a spade lead from East found gold—well, it didn't improve my temper.

"It didn't even help much when Edith Seligman [Edith Kemp] told me afterward that she had made *five notrump* against the spade queen opening at her table. Edith is pretty sharp. She said that she said to herself: "Hmmm, my friend on the left must have a lot of picture cards to get off to a lead like that. Let's try him out." Forthwith, she had led the heart jack through West, and when he covered, she returned to the club ace and finessed again in hearts, against the ten. Succeeding, she promptly dropped West's queen of clubs, and ended up by taking the diamond finesse through West. I guess he had more to complain about than I did."

Deal 4:

I think there is nothing more frustrating in bridge than coming up with the right line of play and losing because on that particular day the fates were against you. Such is the story of the next deal, which might be titled "The Operation Was Successful, but the Patient Died."

The deal arose in the final round of the National Team-of-Four Championship of 1932. The South declarer was the late Walter Malowan.

North-South vulnerable. South dealer.

North

♠ Q 9 5 4
♡ —
◇ 9 8 4 2
♣ A Q 10 8 5

West	East
♠ 6 3 2	♠ J 8 7
♡ A 7 6 3 2	♡ K 9 5
◇ 5	◇ K Q J 10 6
♣ 9 4 3 2	♣ J 6

South

♠ A K 10
♡ Q J 10 8 4
◇ A 7 3
♣ K 7

The bidding:

South	West	North	East
1 ♡	Pass	2 ♣	2 ◇
2 NT	Pass	3 NT	Pass
Pass	Pass		

The bidding may not meet with the reader's approval, but that's the way it went.*

Against the three-notrump contract, West dutifully opened his singleton diamond in response to partner's overcall, Mr. Malowan winning the trick with his ace. He then cashed the ace, king, and queen of spades, each of the opponents following to the first three leads of that suit, and each discarding a heart on the fourth lead. Foremost in declarer's mind, of course, was the question of how he was going to play the club suit, and he was trying to get a "count" of the opponents' cards to help him resolve that question. This is the path his thinking took:

"East, for his two-diamond overcall, obviously has five diamonds. He has followed to three spade leads, and has discarded a heart. I know nine of his original thirteen cards. Four are unknown to me.

"West, on the other hand (no pun intended), has been observed to possess one diamond, three spades, and one heart. Hence, eight of his cards are unknown to me.

"If I took the opponents' twelve unknown cards and shuffled them up, and gave eight to West and four to East, into whose hand would the jack of clubs figure to fall? By two to one odds (eight to four), the knave would fall into the West hand."

On this mathematical logic, at trick six Mr. Malowan led a club to his king, after which he returned his remaining club and finessed dummy's ten-spot. The roof had just caved in. When the opponents got through cashing their winners, Mr. Malowan was three tricks short of his contract.

Mr. Malowan was right in his thinking—West had four clubs and East had but two. By all rights West should have had the jack of clubs, and he would have had it two days out of every three. Today, for Mr. Malowan, was the third day.

Deal 5:

Here is a deal, which, had it been played in a rubber-bridge game, would have been fulfilled by every bridgeplayer in the world. But when it arose in a duplicate game some years ago, most of the South declarers went down—because they took the proper

* When the board was replayed, Oswald Jacoby, sitting in the North seat, reached a four-spade contract. East opened the diamond king, and Jacoby crossruffed the hand for ten tricks.

duplicate percentage play! The hand illustrates the difference between rubber-bridge thinking and duplicate thinking.

East-West vulnerable. East dealer.

North

♠ 9 7 5 3 2
♡ Q
◇ Q 3
♣ A J 8 7 5

West

♠ J
♡ 9 8 6 4 3 2
◇ 10 9
♣ Q 10 9 4

East

♠ K Q
♡ A 10 7
◇ K 7 6 5 4 2
♣ K 2

South

♠ A 10 8 6 4
♡ K J 5
◇ A J 8
♣ 6 3

The bidding:

East	South	West	North
1 ◇	1 ♠	Pass	4 ♠
Pass	Pass	Pass	

West opened the ten of diamonds, which was covered by dummy's queen, East's king, and declarer's ace. Declarer then laid down the trump ace, leaving only the king outstanding.

At rubber bridge, there would be no problem: declarer would give up a spade, a heart, and a club. But at duplicate bridge, the overtrick can be more important than the game itself; and if the odds were right, the safety of the game contract should properly be jeopardized to obtain the overtrick.

The issue, of course, was: who figures to have the *nine* of diamonds? If East has that card, then dummy can be entered via the club ace, and the finesse of declarer's eight of diamonds can be taken. On the ace of diamonds, dummy's singleton heart can now be discarded, thus eliminating a heart loser.

Now, honestly, doesn't East, who bid diamonds, figure to have the nine of diamonds? Wouldn't West have opened the ten of diamonds from the 10 2, the 10 4, the 10 5, the 10 6, or the 10 7?

So declarer entered dummy via the club ace, led the three of diamonds, and inserted his eight-spot. West, as is apparent, won the trick with his nine-spot. And so the defenders cashed four tricks, one in each suit.

Deal 6:

This next deal was one of the recurring nightmares of the late Mike Michaels of Miami Beach, Florida. Before he transplanted himself to that southern clime, Mike was a Washingtonian, and a frequent tournament partner of mine. On this deal, Mike, sitting in the East seat, was the victim of a magnificent deceptive play made by the South declarer.

This is the story of the deal, as told to me by Mike a few hours after it happened in a Washington, D.C., tournament. I have taken the liberty of deleting a few of Mike's "choice" words: when Mike was on the wrong end of things at a bridge table, through no fault of his, he always spoke extemporaneously and spontaneously, with a few unprintable expletives often being inserted into describing how he "wuz robbed."

Neither side vulnerable. North dealer.

North
♠ A 8 7 2
♡ 7 5 3
◇ A 3
♣ K J 10 5

West
♠ 5 4
♡ Q J 9
◇ K 10 8 7
♣ 9 7 4 3

East
♠ Q J 10
♡ K 10 8 2
◇ Q J 9 6
♣ 8 2

South
♠ K 9 6 3
♡ A 6 4
◇ 5 4 2
♣ A Q 6

North	East	South	West
1 ♣	Pass	1 ♠	Pass
2 ♠	Pass	4 ♠	Pass
Pass	Pass		

"My partner, Dickie Freeman, got off to the queen of hearts lead against the four-spade contract, and I gave a 'come-on' with the eight-spot. When declarer permitted the queen to hold the trick, Dickie followed with the heart jack upon which I dropped the deuce, declarer's ace winning.

"South then cashed the ace and king of spades, leaving my high queen outstanding. He now led the ace of clubs, after which he played the six of clubs to dummy's king. Next came the jack of clubs, and I made the automatic, natural play which I would make again today, tomorrow, or in the year 2000. I discarded the six of diamonds—as declarer won the trick with his 'concealed' queen.

"Declarer now reentered dummy via the ace of diamonds and led the ten of clubs. I was a dead duck. No matter whether I trumped or not, declarer would discard his remaining low heart. So declarer made his contract, losing just one heart, one spade, and one diamond.

"Quite obviously, if declarer had played 'normal'—like virtually every other South declarer did—he would have bitten the dust by a trick. That is, after cashing his two top trumps, had he played the ace, *the queen,* and a third club to the board's king, I would have ruffed the third club and cashed my king of hearts. . . . Eventually we would have gotten the setting trick in diamonds.

"It is rather obvious that declarer did a neat job in pulling the wool over my eyes by cashing the ace of clubs, the king of clubs, and then leading the jack of clubs, thus creating the impression that he was going to let the jack ride, hoping that I held the queen (a ruffing finesse). From my position, I *knew* that my partner was going to win the trick with the club queen, and I wasn't going to waste my high queen of trumps on a trick that my partner was sure to win.

"The damned thing about this deal was that it arose in the qualifying round of the Open Pair Championship—and the South declarer who 'swindled' me didn't even qualify for the finals! But he had to pick on me to pull one of the neatest plays of that year—or any other year."

• • •

Deal 7:

To the expert, the execution of a squeeze or an endplay is a commonplace affair, and provides him with no especial thrill. But his joy borders on the ecstatic when he can swindle an opponent, or "steal" a trick from him. The reason behind this attitude is, of course, that a swindle is indicative of the ability to outwit, or outthink his adversary—and to the expert, as to all mortals engaged in competitive endeavors where the thinking process forms the first line of offense—this type of feat is the ultimate in success.

The simple ruse contained in the next deal is a recurring one, and emanates from an ear attuned to the bidding. The South declarer was Alphonse Moyse, Jr. The deal arose in a tournament in 1933.

North-South vulnerable. North dealer.

North

♠ K 10 6 3
♡ Q J
◇ A 6 5
♣ A Q 5 3

West

♠ 5
♡ A 7 6 3
◇ J 9 7 4 2
♣ 7 6 4

East

♠ A 4
♡ 10 9 8 4
◇ K Q 10
♣ K 10 9 2

South

♠ Q J 9 8 7 2
♡ K 5 2
◇ 8 3
♣ J 8

The bidding:

North	East	South	West
1 ♣	1 NT	2 ♠	Pass
3 ♠	Pass	4 ♠	Pass
Pass	Pass		

The analysis of this deal is by Mr. Moyse.

"West opens the ace of hearts and shifts to a diamond. You take stock of the situation and, based on East's one-notrump overcall, decide that the chance of the vital club finesse winning is just about nil. So why take it? You have a much better play available to you—one which *may* win. The ace, and then a low club off dummy. Don't scoff—East is on the spot. He may suspect exactly what you're trying to do, but he can't be sure—you *may* have a singleton, and are hoping that the king will drop on the second or third round of the suit, thereby promoting dummy's queen into a winner. So East has to make a guess—and more than infrequently, he will guess wrong. Your play has everything to gain, and nothing to lose."

Moyse played the hand exactly as presented in the preceding paragraph. At trick three he led the board's ace of clubs, and at trick four, the three of clubs. East thought for a few seconds, crossed his feet, thought for a few more seconds—and then played the nine of clubs!

• • •

Deal 8:

At first glance, this deal may appear to be a "double-dummy" problem.* Actually, it is not. It was played in a tournament in 1938, card for card as is presented below.

Both sides vulnerable. West dealer.

North

♠ A K 9 4 2
♡ A 3
◇ A 6 5
♣ A 7 3

West

♠ 6 3
♡ Q J 10 9 8 7 6 5 4
◇ K
♣ 2

East

♠ 10
♡ —
◇ Q J 10 9 8 4
♣ Q J 10 9 6 5

South

♠ Q J 8 7 5
♡ K 2
◇ 7 3 2
♣ K 8 4

The bidding:

West	North	East	South
4 ♡	Double	Pass	4 ♠
Pass	Pass	Pass	

* For those unfamiliar with the term, double dummy, it means playing out a deal (as a problem) while looking at all fifty-two cards.

West opened the queen of hearts, dummy's ace was put up—and East ruffed with his singleton ten of spades!

At this point the four-spade contract seemed doomed to defeat, since declarer still had one club and two diamond losers. But our super-expert declarer found a way to fulfill his contract on his own power. His beautifully planned solution arose out of the realization that West had started with nine hearts.

When East ruffed dummy's ace of hearts at trick one, declarer followed suit with the *king of hearts!* At trick two, East led the diamond queen, the board's ace capturing the trick, which included West's king of diamonds. Then followed two rounds of trumps, picking up West's pieces, after which a club was led to dummy's ace, West following suit. At this point, declarer knew every one of West's original thirteen cards: nine hearts, two spades, one diamond, and one club.

South now led the dummy's three of hearts, West being forced to win the trick. Since West had nothing but hearts remaining, he had no choice but to lead another heart. On this trick declarer discarded dummy's losing club, while at the same time he discarded a losing diamond from his own hand.

West then led another heart (what else?) which declarer ruffed in dummy while he simultaneously discarded the remaining losing diamond from the South hand. The rest of the tricks now belonged to him, since he was able to crossruff the rest of the hand.

A rather neat problem to solve at the bridge table, don't you think?

chapter **9**

TO TALK OF MANY THINGS, OR THE CHILDREN'S HOUR

Finding a heading for this chapter was a painstaking, time-consuming job, for the chapter consists of a weird potpourri of bridge deals that defy classification. It contains some unbelievable upper-echelon hands, including flights of fancy for which there is no rational explanation, mental aberrations, "blind spots," hunches that backfired, and even an apology from one of the world's greatest players for his handling of a doubled contract.*

And so I was forced to research the title, and I came up with the above. Here is its derivation and its significance:

"To Talk of Many Things" comes from Lewis Carroll's *Through the Looking-Glass:*

> The time has come, the Walrus said,
> To talk of many things:
> Of shoes—and ships—and sealing wax—
> Of cabbages—and kings—
> And why the sea is boiling hot—
> And whether pigs have wings.

"The Children's Hour" is the title of a poem by Henry Wadsworth Longfellow, and the first stanza reads:

> Between the dark and the daylight
> When the night is beginning to lower,
> Comes a pause in the day's occupations,
> That is known as the Children's Hour.

As the reader goes through this chapter, he will understand that the reason for my co-titles is to give him a glimpse into another world, a world seemingly unreal—and yet a real world in which all bridgeplayers find themselves at times, some more than others. The titles (and this introduction) were necessary, I felt, in order to effect the reader's transition from good, expert, adult bridge to . . . the Children's Hour and whether pigs have wings.

* Have *you* ever heard of a topflight player *apologizing* for his play of a hand?

Deal 1:

Virtually all of the deals in this book are concerned with the functioning of the expert mind as it rationally seeks a solution to the specific situation confronting it. In the main, the mind of the expert functions in an orderly, logical way.

At times, however, the mind encounters a blind spot, or perhaps has a temporary aberration which cannot be justified or even explained. The following deal falls into this category. In case the reader, after seeing what happened, comes to the conclusion that the players were beginners, let me state for the record that the deal arose in the World Championships of 1937. The four participants were each of the class of the world's best.

Neither side vulnerable. South dealer.

North
♠ Q 7 2
♡ A K 6 4 3
◇ Q 7
♣ Q 5 4

West
♠ K 10
♡ Q 10
◇ A J 10 3
♣ J 9 8 7 2

East
♠ A
♡ 8 7 5
◇ 8 6 5 4 2
♣ A 10 6 3

South
♠ J 9 8 6 5 4 3
♡ J 9 2
◇ K 9
♣ K

South	West	North	East
Pass	Pass	1 ♡	Pass
1 ♠	Pass	Pass	Pass

Against the one-spade contract West opened the nine (repeat, *nine*) of clubs, dummy played low, as did East, and South's singleton king won the trick. A low diamond was then led toward dummy's queen, West followed with the three-spot, and North's queen captured the trick.

The five of clubs was led next, and East, thinking that South was trying to "steal" his remaining singleton jack, promptly put up the ace—and South, of course, ruffed. South then led a heart to dummy's ace, after which he discarded his king of diamonds on the board's established queen of clubs.

A diamond was now led, South ruffing. If the reader thinks he has seen it all, he is wrong. The climax is yet to come. South's next play was to lead a low trump out of his own hand toward dummy's queen—and great was the fall thereon! West put up his king, which East was compelled to overtake with his singleton ace.

And, in conclusion, when South eventually led his nine of hearts, West's queen fell, promoting South's jack into a winner. With the assistance of the opponents, South thus succeeded in making twelve tricks. His only loser was a trick that couldn't be avoided: to the ace of trumps.

Deal 2:

On occasion, experts have blind spots, even as you and I. Here is a case of a "simple" blind spot—but simple in retrospect only. The narration is by Alphonse Moyse, Jr., and Harry Fishbein.

East-West vulnerable. West dealer.

North
♠ K 10 8 6
♡ A 10 6 3
♢ A 7 3
♣ 8 4

West
♠ Q J 3
♡ J 9 7 2
♢ K Q J 8 4
♣ 6

East
♠ 7 5 2
♡ K Q 5 4
♢ 10 6
♣ 9 5 3 2

South
♠ A 9 4
♡ 8
♢ 9 5 2
♣ A K Q J 10 7

The bidding:

West	North	East	South
Pass	Pass	Pass	1 ♣
Pass	1 ♡	Pass	1 ♠
Pass	4 ♠	Pass	Pass
Pass			

The bidding will not meet with the readers' approval, especially after it is noted that ten tricks are there for the taking at three notrump. The fact, however, is that North and South were two of the nation's top players, Harry Fishbein and Edith Kemp, respectively, and they were playing more or less Roth-Stone, which, on this particular deal, happened to land them in an inferior contract. The deal came up in the National Mixed Pair Championships of 1950.

As Fishbein told the story to Moyse, "West opened the diamond king. Edith called for the ace, then led a club to her ace, and then played the club king." He paused expectantly. "Catch on?"

"Aha!" Moyse said mysteriously, catching nothing.

Sensing Moyse's failure to grasp the situation, Fishbein shouted, "You don't see! West ruffed the club king and cashed two diamonds. But . . ."

"Most unfortunate," Moyse cooed.

"Yeah," said Fishbein. "Edith should have played the *ten* of clubs instead of the king! What West would ruff *that?* . . . Now do you get it?"

Moyse blushed rosily.

"Fishbein was right, of course. Mrs. Kemp had a blind spot, as did Moyse. And the latter was looking at all four hands.

"The difference between the lead of the club king and the club ten at trick three is all the difference in the world, psychologically. *Every* West would ruff the king. Very few—if any—would ruff the ten-spot. And once South slips the ten-spot by, she is sitting pretty. She then leads the club king, and West is fixed, for he now would know that South started with at least the A K Q J 10 of clubs. West would probably ruff the ten-spot with his spade jack (to prevent dummy from discarding too many diamonds) and dummy would overruff with the king."

What would have developed after that is uncertain, but declarer might well have made eleven tricks, depending on how the defenders played. Actually, on this deal, the result is unimportant, since the theme of the hand is "blind spots"—or, perhaps, the imperfection at times of even the expert mind.

Deal 3:

What shakes the confidence of the bridge expert more than any other happening is the reasoned inference that he figured to be right, but which turned out to be wrong. The reader will please note the use of the words, "*shakes* the confidence," not "*shatters* the confidence." As soon as the next deal is about to begin, the nightmare vanishes. But during the moments directly after it came into being, the deluded expert wishes he had not gotten up that morning; or, perhaps, that his partner had stayed in bed. The following deal describes the misfunctioning, or misguessing, of the expert mind.

East-West vulnerable. North dealer.

	North	
	♠ Q J 9 ♡ 7 5 4 3 ◇ Q 9 ♣ K 8 5 2	
West		East
♠ 8 5 3 ♡ A J ◇ A J 8 3 ♣ Q 10 9 4		♠ A 10 6 4 2 ♡ K 10 ◇ 10 7 5 4 ♣ 6 3
	South	
	♠ K 7 ♡ Q 9 8 6 2 ◇ K 6 2 ♣ A J 7	

The bidding:

North	East	South	West
Pass	Pass	1 ♣	Pass
2 ♣	Pass	2 NT	Pass
3 NT	Pass	Pass	Double
Pass	Pass	Pass	

The North-South bidding is virtually impossible to explain—and I'll make no attempt to do so. With respect to West's double of three notrump, it is my guess that he had played against North-South before, and he figured that they had stepped out of line (again).

West chose to open the eight of spades, hoping that his partner had some strength in that suit. The queen was played from dummy, and East paused to analyze the situation.

East couldn't tell whether West's lead was from a doubleton eight or tripleton eight of spades. He finally concluded that whatever it was, he had no chance of establishing his spade suit unless West had the heart suit bottled up; and that, in this case, East's king of hearts would serve as an entry for the cashing of the spade suit. But if West had high-card strength in the heart suit, then it should be a simple matter to establish that suit for his partner.

Having thus reasoned, East won the opening lead with the spade ace and promptly banged down the king of hearts. South false-carded with the nine—and now West came into the act.

From the West seat, it seemed to be a stroke of real luck to have caught his partner with the ace of spades and a heart suit headed by the K Q (sic!). So West, showing wonderful partnership rapport, made haste to establish East's heart suit by unblocking: he overtook the king with his ace, and then led the jack of hearts!

Declarer's contracted-for nine tricks were now there for the taking, by giving up a diamond. The fact that he eventually made an extra trick (by endplaying West and forcing the latter to lead a club) is unimportant, for no other North-South pair made as much as three notrump doubled.

Had East declined to capture the opening spade lead, then when West regained the lead (in hearts), he would have played another spade, East again declining to win his ace. When West would subsequently have obtained the lead again, he would have returned his remaining spade, and East would have cashed his spade suit. Played in this fashion, the defenders would have made three spade tricks, two hearts, and the diamond ace, inflicting a two-trick set on declarer.

Deal 4:

This deal has nothing to do with the play of the cards as such, but it does serve to illustrate the spur-of-the-moment agile thinking of the expert mind when a problem related to the play of the cards arises.

The hand, which arose in a tournament, was one of the reasons for changing the section of the 1935 Laws of Contract Bridge that pertained to "claiming the balance of the tricks." The deal became known as "the seven of clubs finesse."

Neither side vulnerable. North dealer.

North

♠ A Q 6
♡ 4
◇ 9 6 3
♣ A K Q 8 7 2

West

♠ 10 7
♡ K 10 5 2
◇ 8 7 2
♣ J 10 9 6

East

♠ 9 8 5 4 2
♡ A Q 8 6
◇ K Q 10 5
♣ —

South

♠ K J 3
♡ J 9 7 3
◇ A J 4
♣ 5 4 3

The bidding:

North	East	South	West
1 ♣	Double	1 NT	Pass
3 NT	Pass	Pass	Pass

West opened the deuce of hearts, and the defenders rattled off four heart tricks. As that ended the heart suit, South tossed his cards face up on the table, remarking: "That's all." West studied the North-South cards for a moment, then said: "How are you going to play it?" Without a moment's hesitation, South retorted: "I'm going to finesse the seven of clubs."

It was obvious to all concerned that the quick-witted South player had realized that West could dispute the claim only if he held all four outstanding clubs. Although the director ruled * that South must give up at least another trick, South made out a fair legalistic case under the existing law as to why he should be permitted to finesse.

In the new code that came came out in 1943, the law was revised to forestall any such display of mental agility. One clause now read that "unless declarer's intention . . . was announced before or coincident with the facing of his hand . . ." the defenders can direct the play and forbid the taking of finesses.†

Deal 5:

Without a doubt, the most abused artificial bid in bridge is the Blackwood Slam Convention. By and large, this convention is used quite promiscuously, with the result that many unmakable slams are arrived at (even with the partnership possessing all four aces); or, where the responder shows an insufficient number of aces to warrant being in a slam, the partnership stops at five hearts or five spades, and suffers a one-trick set. And, as the reader appreciates—possibly through a recollection of similar bitter experiences—there is nothing more disheartening than getting to five hearts or five spades on your own power—and going down a trick.

* The deal arose in 1942.

† As an added bit of protection, the current laws state ". . . the director should not permit declarer to take advantage of any information gained subsequent to his claim. . . ."

Basically, the Blackwood Slam Convention is not a device that is used to get you to a slam—it is a device that is used *to keep you out of a slam.* From the expert's point of view, the Blackwood Convention is brought into application when he has been more or less convinced by the preceding bidding sequence that the partnership holdings warrant being in a slam *provided the opponents don't have two cashable aces;* and he then bids "four notrump" as a check-up gadget, to make sure he doesn't land in a slam missing a couple of aces.

On rare occasions, the Blackwood Slam Convention is employed by the expert in a paradoxical fashion: to make sure that *his partner* does not drive either to an unmakable slam or to an inferior five-level contract in hearts or spades. Here is a case in point. The South declarer was Alfred Sheinwold, world-renowned authority and player. I was sitting North. The deal arose in the National Men's Pair Championship held in Washington, D.C., in 1961. The narration is by Mr. Sheinwold.

Both sides vulnerable. North dealer.

North

♠ K Q 9 6
♡ A K 3
◇ K 6 3 2
♣ 7 5

West

♠ 8
♡ Q 9 8 6
◇ 7
♣ K Q 10 9 6 4 2

East

♠ J 10 7 5 4 2
♡ 7 2
◇ 9 8 5
♣ A 3

South

♠ A 3
♡ J 10 5 4
◇ A Q J 10 4
♣ J 8

The bidding:

North	East	South	West
1 ♢	Pass	1 ♡	3 ♣*
Pass	Pass	3 ♠	Pass
4 ♠	Pass	4 NT	Pass
5 ♢	Pass	Pass	Pass

"When Fred opened the bidding with one diamond the future looked bright (little did I realize how quickly I would change my mind). My one-heart response was normal—we were not opening four-card major suits in first or second position, and my partner might well have held four hearts. West's preemptive three-club overcall achieved its desired effect—it deprived us of bidding space. North passed, not having a logical or comfortable bid to make; and East did likewise, with no strain whatever. I now had a problem.

"As I viewed it, three notrump might well be our best contract, provided, of course, that my partner had the clubs stopped. So, taking a calculated risk, I now bid my magnificent two-card spade suit, hoping that my partner would bid three notrump if he could stop the clubs.

"Unfortunately, my calculated risk backfired: Fred properly raised me to four spades. East passed serenely, and it was up to me to find a way out of the trap.

"I knew that if I bid five diamonds (where I wanted to rest), Fred would take me back to five spades (or, possibly, hearts) since nobody plays minor suit game contracts in tournaments (spades and hearts count 30 points per trick; clubs and diamonds, 20 per trick).

"With no intention of getting to a slam, and hoping that Fred held just one ace, I now made the Blackwood bid of four notrump. It was a lovely day: Fred bid five diamonds, after which it went pass, pass, pass.

"From here in, the sailing was smooth and pleasurable. The opponents took their two club tricks, and that was that. Since the

* The weak jump overcall.

finesse for the heart queen was successful, we made the remaining eleven tricks and our contract.

"As to what I would have done if Fred had bid five hearts over four notrump, that's easy to answer. I would have bid six diamonds, with my fingers crossed. If this answer does not satisfy the reader, I will delightedly listen to any alternative, rational solution. (But, please, don't say: 'You should not have bid three spades.' That advice I could have used *before* I made that bid, not after.)"

Deal 6:

As a change of pace, I would like to introduce the following humorous deal, which portrays not the functioning of the expert mind, but rather the malfunctioning of the nonexpert mind. The theme of this deal is one which is familiar to all bridgeplayers: never concede defeat until every possibility of making a contract has been exhausted (including the hope that the opponents, even as you and I, sometimes have blind spots; or they might revoke, etc.). On occasions a squeeze can be developed—as on this deal—even if declarer doesn't know a thing about a squeeze play. The hand arose in a duplicate game in 1932.

Both sides vulnerable. South dealer.

	North	
	♠ A K J 10 6	
	♡ A 2	
	◇ K J	
	♣ K J 10 3	
West		East
♠ Q 7 4		♠ 9 8 5
♡ J 10 9 3		♡ Q 8 7 6 4
◇ 10 7 6 4 2		◇ 3
♣ 9		♣ 8 6 5 2
	South	
	♠ 3 2	
	♡ K 5	
	◇ A Q 9 8 5	
	♣ A Q 7 4	

The bidding:

South	West	North	East
1 ◇	Pass	2 ♠	Pass
3 ♣	Pass	4 ♣	Pass
4 NT	Pass	7 NT	Pass
Pass	Pass		

West opened the jack of hearts, and after dummy was put down, South exposed his cards, saying: "I have all thirteen tricks—two spades, two hearts, five diamonds, and four clubs." Whereupon West, after examining the North-South hands, screamed for the director, who, being told of South's statement, informed South: "You must play out this hand without taking any finesses."

South won the opening heart lead with dummy's ace, after which he cashed the king and jack of diamonds. When East discarded a heart on the second diamond lead, South realized that he could not make five diamond tricks. Since he was barred from taking the spade finesse, he then laid down the ace and king of spades. When the queen failed to drop, South conceded that he was down one.

In experience, one learns never to claim a contract, for in claiming he stands to break even or to lose, never to gain. Just about invariably, the opponents contest the claim, so that not even time is gained.

However, from our South declarer's position, once he had made the claim and West disputed it, it should have been apparent that West had the diamond suit protected and he also figured to have the guarded queen of spades. Armed with this knowledge, South could have fulfilled his grand-slam contract without the spade finesse, in this simple fashion:

After winning the opening heart lead with dummy's ace, South should have cashed the king and jack of diamonds (revealing the already-known "bad news"). Now the ace of spades would be played, after which four rounds of clubs would be taken, ending up in the South hand. Next the ace and queen of diamonds would be cashed, and this position would be arrived at:

North

♠ K J
♡ 2
◇ —
♣ —

West	East
♠ Q 7	♠ 9
♡ —	♡ Q 8
◇ 10	◇ —
♣ —	♣ —

South

♠ 3
♡ K
◇ 9
♣ —

To trick eleven, the king of hearts would be led, and West would be squeezed: if he discarded the seven of spades, the board's king and jack would win the last two tricks; if, instead, he tossed away the diamond ten, declarer's nine of diamonds and dummy's king of spades would yield declarer his grand slam.

South had a chance to be a hero—but he failed to make the grade.

Deal 7:

All bridgeplayers—expert and nonexpert alike—are frequently forced to guess as to how to play out a hand. And when one finds himself in this position, he inevitably must misguess at times, although the nonexpert is more prone to guess wrong than is the expert.

Here is a deal where a world-renowned expert, Theodore A. Lightner, was confronted with a guess that an inferior player would probably have resolved correctly in short order because the latter would not have taken all the facts into consideration. But Mr. Lightner, after a lengthy deliberation of the total evidence, came up with the "wrong view." The deal was played in the Summer National Championships of 1940.

East-West vulnerable. North dealer.

North

♠ J 10 3
♡ A K J
◇ A 8 5
♣ A 10 8 3

West

♠ K 8 2
♡ 8 7 6 4
◇ 9 6
♣ Q J 9 7

East

♠ 7 5
♡ Q 9 3 2
◇ 10 7 4 3 2
♣ 6 4

South

♠ A Q 9 6 4
♡ 10 5
◇ K Q J
♣ K 5 2

The bidding:

North	East	South	West
1 NT	Pass	3 ♠	Pass
4 ◇	Pass	6 ◇	Pass
6 ♠	Pass	Pass	Pass

Sitting West was General Robert Gill, while East was Claggett Bowie. North was Oswald Jacoby and Theodore Lightner was the South declarer.

It took General Gill a long time to make his opening lead against the six-spade contract. When it came out, it was the queen of clubs. Declarer took this with his king, after which he entered dummy via the heart ace to take the spade finesse. When West won with his king, he promptly returned the seven of clubs. Mr. Lightner now had his problem.

Normally, the blind lead of a queen at trick one denotes possession of the jack. In this case, however, Lightner was not at all sure, for West's lead, after a prolonged deliberation, might well have been from a Q x doubleton. In point of fact, Mr. Lightner did come to the conclusion that the lead had been from a doubleton. So he went up with the board's club ace, led a trump to his nine, and took the heart finesse. Had it worked, he would have been able to discard his losing club on dummy's top heart. Unfortunately, the finesse lost to East's queen, and Mr. Lightner was down one.

Another factor that undoubtedly motivated Mr. Lightner into declining to finesse dummy's club ten was that if a club lead had not been made initially, declarer would have had no play for his contract except to resort to the heart finesse. So rather than attempting to mastermind whether General Gill's lead had been a normal or abnormal one, he asked himself the question: "How would I have played the hand if a club had not been opened?" The answer was, of course, "I'd take the heart finesse."

As was stated, the inexpert declarer would probably have fulfilled the slam, for he would have accepted the lead of the club queen at face value, and would have finessed the board's ten of clubs at trick four. And do you know what? He would have made the winning play.

In conclusion, from a technical point of view. With North having opened the bidding with one notrump, an opening lead by West from Q J x or Q J x x figured to be a losing lead more often than not. I assume that Mr. Lightner assumed that General Gill was not unaware of this "statistic". Yet, the lead of the queen from a doubleton Q x figured to be a worse lead. I assume Mr. Lightner assumed General Gill also realized that . . . etc., etc.

Deal 8:

Back in 1941, in the Eastern Championships, virtually every South player arrived at a four-spade contract on the next deal. Most of them went down, the reason, as they put it, being, "How could we have foreseen such miserable distribution?" In a theoretical sense, they were right—the distribution was unexpectedly abnormal. But, in a practical sense, they were wrong, for they could have overcome it, and come home safely with all the marbles. Here is the deal.

Both sides vulnerable. South dealer.

North

♠ 6 5
♡ J 9 8 4 3 2
◇ K 8
♣ J 7 3

West	**East**
♠ J	♠ 10 9 3 2
♡ Q 10 6 5	♡ K
◇ 5 2	◇ J 10 7 6 4
♣ Q 10 8 5 4 2	♣ A K 6

South

♠ A K Q 8 7 4
♡ A 7
◇ A Q 9 3
♣ 9

The bidding:

South	West	North	East
1 ♠	Pass	1 NT	Pass
4 ♠	Pass	Pass	Pass

The above was the bidding sequence at most of the tables. West got off to a club lead, East taking his king and continuing with the ace, which South ruffed.

With a view toward ruffing the losing diamond, the various declarers then played a diamond to the board's king, returned a diamond to South's ace, and then led the diamond nine. As can be observed, West ruffed the third diamond with the singleton jack—and our declarers had just gone down, since there was no way they could avoid the loss of a heart and a trump trick.

Admittedly, it was a bit of tough luck to have run into West having not only a doubleton diamond but also a singleton spade. Nevertheless, the contract could easily have been fulfilled—as it was by one declarer, who explained his play thusly:

"After I ruffed East's ace of clubs, I cashed the king and ace of diamonds. I figured it would cost me absolutely nothing to now lay down my ace of trumps, to minimize the chances of one of the opponents ruffing the third round of diamonds. As it happened, I luckily caught West's singleton jack. I then led my nine of diamonds and ruffed it.

"I thought the result would be an average one, and I was frankly quite surprised when the scores were posted to note that we had obtained ten match points out of twelve."

Our declarer's analysis was masterful, especially the phrase "I figured it would cost me nothing to now lay down my ace of trumps. . . ." Of such stuff are victors made.

Deal 9:

One of the greatest players this world has ever known is B. Jay Becker of New York City. Through the decades, his feats at the bridge table have thrilled both the onlookers and the readers to whom his exploits were presented. To the best of my knowledge, no criticism of his technique has appeared in print, due primarily to the fact that his mistakes are few and far between. In the following deal, he is criticized for having had a blind spot—and the critic is none other than B. Jay himself! Here is his story, concerning a deal which he played in the Vanderbilt Cup Championships of 1950. He was sitting South.

Both sides vulnerable. North dealer.

North

♠ A 10 2
♡ Q 5 3
◇ K 5 3 2
♣ 9 4 3

West

♠ K
♡ A J 9 4
◇ A J 10 8 6
♣ K 7 5

East

♠ 7 5 4
♡ K 10 8 6 2
◇ 9 7
♣ J 10 8

South

♠ Q J 9 8 6 3
♡ 7
◇ Q 4
♣ A Q 6 2

The bidding:

North	East	South	West
Pass	Pass	1 ♠	Double
2 ♠	Pass	Pass	3 ◇
Pass	3 ♡	Pass	4 ♡
Double	Pass	4 ♠	Double
Pass	Pass	Pass	

B. Jay commented that in view of the way the bidding developed, he had been sorry that he hadn't bid three spades on the second round, but that at least he had saved something by taking out the double of four hearts, since East could have made that contract without much trouble.

"West laid down the diamond ace, and East fumbled a little,

then played the seven-spot," said Becker, "so I knew—and so did West—that East had two diamonds. West cashed the ace of hearts and then led the heart jack through dummy. I ruffed and pushed the spade queen through West. He covered with the king, and I won with dummy's ace. What should I play next?

"I didn't do the right thing, but I had no excuse for missing the correct play. South *must* ruff dummy's last heart at this point! Then he cashes the spade jack and the diamond queen, and goes back to dummy with a spade to the ten. Meanwhile, do you see what happens to West? He can give up a diamond on the second spade lead, but when the third spade is led, he can't afford to give up anything except a heart, his last one. If he throws a club, South should certainly read his exact holding and knock out the club king by playing the ace of clubs, followed by a low club, thereby promoting South's two remaining clubs into winners.

"So, with West out of hearts, South has a cinch. He throws one club on the diamond king and another club on dummy's last diamond, which he lets West win. Then West has to lead a club up to the ace queen.

"The funny thing was," B. Jay concluded sadly, "that, at the time, I simply couldn't see the value of ruffing dummy's last heart. I thought about it, but it looked as though I was just using up a trump and could get the same effect by running trumps later. I wound up losing a heart, a diamond, and two clubs."

Deal 10:

Here is a seven-notrump contract that I believe every player in the world would fulfill without any stress or strain in about five seconds flat (or an approximation thereto). Our actual declarer, Charles J. Solomon of Philadelphia, who is acknowledged to be one of our nation's leading players, also fulfilled the contract, but it was quite an ordeal for him—and for his partner, Lee Hazen.

The deal arose in the Masters Individual Championship of 1941, which, incidentally, was won by Mr. Hazen. The narration and analysis of the circumstances of the deal are by Mr. Hazen.

"The hand that gave me the biggest chill (that's no typographical error) was one played with Charlie Solomon as my partner against Bobby McPherran and Mrs. Emily Folline in the second session.

North-South vulnerable. East dealer.

North

♠ 9 8 7
♡ K 8 4
♢ K 10 9 7 4 2
♣ A

West

♠ Q 10 5
♡ 2
♢ J 8 6 3
♣ K 10 7 5 4

East

♠ 6 3 2
♡ J 9 7 6 3
♢ —
♣ Q J 8 3 2

South

♠ A K J 4
♡ A Q 10 5
♢ A Q 5
♣ 9 6

The bidding:

East	South	West	North
Pass	1 ♠	Pass	2 ♢
Pass	3 ♡	Pass	4 ♣
Pass	4 ♢	Pass	4 ♡
Pass	5 NT	Pass	7 NT
Pass	Pass	Pass	

"The bidding was rather aggressive but the contract was a good percentage one. Whether you're playing rubber bridge or duplicate, the bidding of a grand slam always generates an air of tension, and this was no exception. After some thought, McPherran led a club, which was won in dummy. Charlie now studied and saw that the contract was cold if the hearts broke or the spade finesse worked. He led a small diamond from dummy to the ace, and when Mrs. Folline showed out, broke out in a cold sweat (at least, that is what it looked like to me). I didn't know what his problem was, but if he was worried, so was I! I began to bitterly regret my bidding, and began thinking of explanations to give an irate partner. For a moment, I thought that when he bawled me out, I would say that this or that bid had been a slip of the tongue or that I had thought he was playing Blackwood or something.

"Charlie now cashed the diamond queen, the heart ace, the spade king, and led a small heart to dummy. When Bobby showed out, the finesse for the jack was proved, and taken back to the closed hand, the ten-spot winning. At this point, McPherran looked puzzled. He showed me his hand and it was obvious that all the tricks were ours. I couldn't understand why Charlie didn't claim them, but then it dawned on me that he must have miscounted the diamonds (thinking that McPherran had five to the jack, instead of the actual four).

"Now I redoubled Charlie's cold sweat. I could easily foresee his taking a losing spade finesse. He cashed the last heart and discarded a spade, and then exclaimed 'I am a dope!' and spread the hand as he announced, 'Bobby, I'm finessing you for the diamond jack.' "

Deal 11*:

I am not certain as to whether this next deal depicts the functioning of the expert mind, but I have the feeling that it probably does. At any rate, the reader can judge for himself. The narration of the deal is shared by Lee Hazen and Richard Frey.

"Did I tell you," Lee asked, "about the hand which first led me to suspect that my wife was a great bridgeplayer?"

* From *The Bridge World*, September 1943.

Both sides vulnerable. North dealer.

North

♠ A Q
♡ J 9 5
◇ Q J 8 6
♣ J 10 7 4

West

♠ 9 8 4
♡ Q 7 6 2
◇ A 5 3
♣ A 9 5

East

♠ K 10 7 6 5
♡ 10 4 3
◇ 9 2
♣ 8 3 2

South

♠ J 3 2
♡ A K 8
◇ K 10 7 4
♣ K Q 6

The bidding:

North	East	South	West
Pass	Pass	1 NT	Pass
3 NT	Pass	Pass	Pass

"I was West, and the better half of our pair was, luckily for me, sitting East. Picking out the card nearest my left thumb, I led the nine of spades. Of course dummy played the queen—and what do you suppose the little genius did? Yessir, she played the seven-spot!

"The declarer set about the establishment of the diamonds. I won the ace and led another spade which knocked out dummy's ace. As you see, declarer couldn't possibly run nine tricks without winning some clubs, and when I got in again with the club ace and led my last spade, Mrs. H. calmly gathered in three spade tricks. Need I point out that if she had won the first spade trick with the king—an obvious temptation which would have proved irresistible to any average player—nothing in the world would have given her a re-entry."

"Lee," said Dick Frey, "that is truly a fine play. The only other time I have seen anything like it was when a player pulled the wrong card. May I ask you a question?"

"Absolutely not!" Hazen said hastily.

chapter **10**

THE MASTERY OF TECHNIQUE

"Technique," according to the dictionary definition, means "technical skill, practically applied, especially in artistic work." It is in this context that the word technique is used within this chapter.

However, I would like to qualify and extend this definition, and make it more inclusive. By "the mastery of technique" is not meant merely a thorough familiarity with all of the principles of sound declarer's play and defense (percentage plays, safety plays, signals, etc.) and with all of the advanced situations that require both special treatment and a judicious, delicate touch (endplays, squeezes, coups, etc.). In addition, my definition encompasses the application of deceptive tactics when the situation calls for it; an acute awareness at all times of the opponents' bidding and its significance; and the presence of table judgment as a factor that can often outweigh the proper mathematical probabilities. All in all, by "mastery of technique" I mean its correct application by "the complete bridge-player," as limited only by innate human frailty.

The twelve deals contained in this chapter will, I believe, give the reader a kaleidoscopic view of "genius at work," or at least a reasonable facsimile thereof.

Deal 1:

If I had to select just one deal to illustrate to a group of novices how the mind of the bridge expert functions, I believe I would choose the one which follows. It is a classic deal, and came up in a

Philadelphia duplicate game back in the early thirties. The actual bidding presented below may be subject to criticism, but I doubt that any alternative sequence would be more acceptable.

Both sides vulnerable. East dealer.

North
♠ 8 7 4
♡ Q 8 7
◇ 8 7 3
♣ 8 6 5 2

West
♠ 9 5 3
♡ 6
◇ 9 6 5 2
♣ J 9 7 4 3

East
♠ K J 10 2
♡ K 5 2
◇ K J 10
♣ K Q 10

South
♠ A Q 6
♡ A J 10 9 4 3
◇ A Q 4
♣ A

The bidding:

East	South	West	North
1 NT	3 ♡	Pass	4 ♡
Pass	Pass	Pass	

West's four of clubs opening lead was won by South's singleton ace. It was perfectly obvious to South that East, for his vulnerable one notrump opening bid had, amongst other high cards, the four outstanding kings. It was equally apparent that East, by definition, had a balanced hand, which meant that each of his kings was guarded. With these "facts" serving as the foundation, declarer went about his business.

At trick two South led the jack of trumps and overtook it with dummy's queen, East winning with the king. East returned a club, declarer ruffing with the ten, after which he led the four of hearts and took it with the board's eight-spot. The diamond finesse was now taken, successfully. Next the three of trumps was led to dummy's seven-spot, and a spade was led, declarer's queen being finessed. At the end, declarer conceded a spade and a diamond.

In terms of approach, declarer knew that both finesses—in spades and diamonds—would be successful. The problem was to be able to get to dummy two times to take the finesses. If the ace of trumps were cashed at any time, declarer would have but one entry, since East's trump king was bound to be a sure winner. Further, if declarer had ruffed with either the three or four of hearts (at trick three), he would have lost an entry to dummy, since both of these cards were essential for gaining access to the board's seven and eight of trumps.

The proper play of this hand required neither brilliance nor genius. All that was needed was a marshaling of the facts available (derived from the bidding) and the practical application of the knowledge obtained.

Deal 2:

If I were asked to select just one deal to illustrate that no deal, no matter how simple, can be played correctly unless utmost consideration is given to the opponents' bidding, I would select the one that follows. Frankly, if I submitted this deal to all of the world's players, neglecting to introduce the opponents' bidding, and asked them how they would play the grand-slam contract, virtually every player would go down! But with the bidding of the opponents being presented, all of our topnotch players would easily fulfill the contract. As to how below-topnotch players would fare if the adverse bidding were not withheld from them, I will not venture to surmise, although I would wager that the majority would fail to fulfill the grand-slam contract.

When the deal arose in the All-West Championships of 1950,

held at Los Angeles, our South declarer, Robert Marks, had no trouble in bringing his contract home safely.

North-South vulnerable. South dealer.

North

♠ Q 7
♡ J 10 5
◊ A 10 8 4 2
♣ 10 9 6

West

♠ 9 6 5
♡ 9 8 6
◊ —
♣ A 8 7 5 4 3 2

East

♠ J 8 4 3 2
♡ 3
◊ J 9 5 3
♣ K Q J

South

♠ A K 10
♡ A K Q 7 4 2
◊ K Q 7 6
♣ —

The bidding:

South	West	North	East
2 ♡	4 ♣	4 ◊	Pass
5 ♣	Pass	5 ♡	Pass
7 ♡	Pass	Pass	Pass

West opened the ace of clubs, which Bob ruffed in the South hand, after which he drew three rounds of trumps. Next he cashed the ace of spades—and then stopped to take inventory.

In all probability, West figured to have seven or eight clubs for his preemptive jump to four clubs, although the possibility existed that he might have but six clubs. West had followed to three rounds of trumps, and also to the lead of the spade ace. Therefore, without any doubt, ten of West's cards were absolutely known to declarer: six clubs, three hearts, and one spade. Hence, *West could not possibly possess the four outstanding diamonds,* headed of course, by the jack.

It is obviously apparent to the reader that the above thoughts, as they circulated through declarer's mind, were for the purpose of determining how to play the diamond suit, the worry being that one of the opponents might have all four of the missing diamonds. Normally, in the abstract, the tendency would be to lead the king, thus trapping West if the latter possessed the J 9 5 3. But, in this case, it was proven that West could not have the four outstanding diamonds; and, therefore, the only one who could have the four of them (if anybody did) was East. Therefore, declarer's play had to be designed to guard against East's possession of the four diamonds.

And so, after cashing the spade ace at trick five, declarer led the six of diamonds to the board's ace—and was pleasantly rewarded when West discarded a club. The ten of diamonds was then returned, East covered with the jack, and declarer won the trick with the queen.

Dummy was now reentered via the spade queen, and the eight of diamonds was led. It won the trick when East followed with the three-spot (had East covered with the nine, declarer would have captured the trick with his king, and his seven-spot would at that moment have become the highest diamond left in the deck). Declarer now exposed his hand, and claimed the remainder of the tricks.

It is apparent that if declarer's first diamond lead had been the king or queen, he would have gone down, being compelled eventually to lose a diamond trick to East's jack.

Deal 3:

One of the strong points of the bridge expert's game—like the master chessplayer's game—is his ability to look ahead and visualize what will develop if he adopts Plan A, or Plan B, or Plan C, etc. As he thinks out the expected consequences of each of these different plans, he discards the least efficient ones, and adopts the one that offers him the greatest chance of success. Quite often, he comes up with the perfect solution; but, just as often, he is forced to accept the better of what is available, with no absolute guarantee that it will bring victory. Here is a deal that illustrates this point.

Both sides vulnerable. South dealer.

North

♠ Q 10 9
♡ A 6 2
◇ 8 4 2
♣ K J 7 4

West

♠ A 6
♡ K 10 9 8 4 3
◇ A 7 5
♣ 8 2

East

♠ 7 5 4 3 2
♡ J
◇ 10 9 6 3
♣ 6 5 3

South

♠ K J 8
♡ Q 7 5
◇ K Q J
♣ A Q 10 9

The bidding:

South	West	North	East
1 NT	2 ♡	2 NT	Pass
3 NT	Pass	Pass	Pass

West opened the ten of hearts, the deuce was played from dummy, East put up his jack—and a bell rang in South's head that said "Time Out." Here are South's thoughts as he surveyed the lay of the land.

"For his vulnerable two-heart overcall against my strong one-notrump opening, West certainly has a six-card heart suit headed by the king, plus the two outside aces. If I capture East's jack with my queen, and drive out the first of his aces—let's say, spades—then he will return a heart, removing my last stopper in his suit. Now when I knock out his other ace—in diamonds—he will cash his established heart suit, and inflict a one-trick set on me. Thus, if I win the opening lead, I am doomed to defeat.

"But if I allow East's jack of hearts to win the opening lead, East will be unable to play back a heart—he has no more.* Whatever else he returns, I will have obtained the 'timing' to knock out West's aces—and I will still have my two stoppers in hearts against *West's* leads of that suit."

Having thus reasoned, South permitted East's jack of hearts to capture the opening lead. East elected to play back the ten of diamonds, and South's king fell to West's ace. West came back with a diamond, which was taken by declarer's queen (had West come back with a heart, he would have given declarer an overtrick). South now led his king of spades, West taking the ace. South had just fulfilled his contract—two spades, one heart, two diamonds, and four clubs.

Because of South's refusal to win the opening heart lead, he restricted himself to just one heart winner—but he fulfilled his contract. Had he won the opening heart lead, he would have made two heart tricks—but his nine-trick contract would have then become unattainable.

In bridge, "counting" is always with you: you count your points in bidding; in the play, you count your winning and losing tricks; you count trumps when you are the declarer, so that you can draw the outstanding adverse trumps; when the rubber has ended, you count your score, etc., etc. But there is another type of counting in bridge known as "counting out a hand." By "counting out a hand" is

* I am sure declarer realized that if East possessed a doubleton jack of hearts (assuming West held only five hearts), then declarer was predestined to defeat, for there would, in this case, be no way to avoid the loss of three heart tricks and the two outstanding aces.

meant trying to reconstruct the original suit distribution of the opponents' cards, the general purpose being to enable you to determine "scientifically" which of two or three optional lines of play is the proper percentage play.

Years ago, counting out a hand was assumed by the average player to be too difficult to absorb, and it was a subject that was considered to be for experts only. But, in the words of Tennyson, just as "the old order changeth, yielding place to new," so counting out a hand has now become public property, and is not nearly so difficult as the reader might have been led to believe.

Let us now examine three deals in which counting out a hand provided the key to success.

Deal 4:

On this first deal, declarer's count led him to the play that gave him his best chance to fulfill a slam contract. It failed only because West also was in there, counting.

East-West vulnerable. North dealer.

North

♠ A Q 6 3
♡ Q J 8
◇ 9 3 2
♣ A 8 4

West

♠ —
♡ 10 9 6 3 2
◇ K J 10 6 5 4
♣ K Q

East

♠ 5 4 2
♡ 7 5
◇ Q
♣ J 10 9 7 6 5 2

South

♠ K J 10 9 8 7
♡ A K 4
◇ A 8 7
♣ 3

The bidding:

North	East	South	West
1 ♣	Pass	2 ♠	Pass
4 ♠	Pass	4 NT	Pass
5 ♡	Pass	6 ♠	Pass
Pass	Pass		

When South won the opening lead of the king of clubs with dummy's ace, he immediately ruffed a low club, returned to dummy with a trump and ruffed North's last club. Two more trump leads gathered in East's trumps. The ace and king of hearts were cashed next, after which South took a time out for inventory.

East was known to have started with seven clubs and three spades (West had failed to follow to the third lead of clubs, and had started with notrumps). Since East had followed to two rounds of hearts, that left only one unknown card in his hand. If it were another heart (meaning that West had the K Q J 10 x x x of diamonds), South had no chance to escape losing two diamond tricks. South's only hope was that East's unknown card was a diamond big enough to win the first diamond trick. If such were the case, East would have to lead a club and South could then discard a diamond while he trumped the trick in dummy.

But if South cashed his last heart before leading a low diamond, East, if he were on his toes, could escape the throw-in by getting rid of his dangerous diamond. So declarer now led a low diamond out of his hand.

It would have been so easy for the West defender—the late Harry Merkle—to have slipped and not to have left himself open to criticism. All he had to do was to play the ten or jack of diamonds, topping dummy's nine. Had he done this, East would have been compelled to capture the trick with his singleton queen—and to return a club upon which declarer would have discarded his other losing diamond while trumping the trick in dummy.

But Mr. Merkle was doing some counting of his own, along with declarer. He, too, knew that East had started with seven clubs, two hearts, and three spades. And he knew, in addition, that East probably held the singleton queen of diamonds, for if declarer had held that card he would have led a diamond off dummy, rather than from his own hand. So Mr. Merkle "expended" the king of diamonds on South's lead of a low diamond, felling his partner's queen. He then continued with the diamond jack, and subsequently took the setting trick with his ten of diamonds.

From where I sit, this was magnificent all-around play. It's just too bad there had to be a loser.

Deal 5:

In the Canadian-American Championships of 1939, one of Canada's leading players, D. G. J. Farquharson, did a simple but neat job of counting out the opponents' cards. His expert thinking earned him a tie-for-top on the deal.

Both sides vulnerable. North dealer.

North

♠ 7 2
♡ A 6
◇ K 9 4
♣ A K J 9 6 3

West

♠ K 4
♡ K 10 8 4 3
◇ J 6 3
♣ Q 10 8

East

♠ A Q 8 6 5
♡ Q 9 5 2
◇ 10 7 5
♣ 5

South

♠ J 10 9 3
♡ J 7
◇ A Q 8 2
♣ 7 4 2

The bidding:

North	East	South	West
1 ♣	1 ♠	1 NT	Pass
3 NT	Pass	Pass	Pass

West dutifully led the king of spades and followed up by playing the four of spades, East's queen winning. It was obvious to East (as it was to declarer) that West had started with exactly two spades. Had he held three originally, he would have led his third highest.

At trick three, East shifted to the deuce of hearts, declarer played the jack, and West's king was captured by the board's ace. East's shift to the deuce of hearts was most revealing to declarer, for it informed him that an "honest" East was leading his fourth-highest heart; and, hence, that the latter possessed exactly four hearts.

After cashing dummy's ace of clubs, Mr. Farquharson then led his three top diamonds, ending up in the South hand. This was done to get a complete count of the opponents' cards. When East followed to all three leads, his hand had became an open book: five spades, four hearts, three diamonds, and one club (the latter had been played when dummy's ace of clubs was cashed).

Thus, after cashing the thirteenth diamond and discarding dummy's remaining heart, declarer finessed against West's marked queen of clubs, thereby making two overtricks.

• • •

Deal 6:

A very good friend of mine, George Beynon, prominent bridge authority and tournament director, died in June 1965. George had reached his one hundredth birthday the preceding September. During the last thirty-four years of his life, bridge was his vocation and his avocation. When he was ninety-eight years old, he was still driving more than one hundred miles virtually every other weekend to play in some tournament.

On his one hundredth birthday, his friends gave a party for him, and quite naturally a duplicate game was part of the entertainment. Here is one of the hands George played that day.

Both sides vulnerable. South dealer.

North

♠ Q J 10 9
♡ K 7 3
♢ A Q J
♣ A 10 2

West	**East**
♠ K 7 5	♠ 6 2
♡ J 10 9 8 6 4	♡ 5
♢ 9 7 3	♢ 8 5 4 2
♣ 6	♣ Q 9 8 7 4 3

South

♠ A 8 4 3
♡ A Q 2
♢ K 10 6
♣ K J 5

The bidding:

South	West	North	East
1 NT	Pass	6 NT	Pass
Pass	Pass		

West opened the jack of hearts, which George won with dummy's king. He then took the spade finesse, losing to West's king. West returned the ten of hearts, declarer's queen winning as East discarded the two of diamonds.

George now cashed three rounds of spades and three rounds of diamonds. A club was then led to the board's ace, after which the deuce of clubs was played back. At this point George turned to East and said: "Nancy, you have the queen of clubs and I'm going to finesse you for it."

When East followed with a low club, George inserted his jack, which won the trick. The slam was now there for the taking.

How did George know that East held the club queen? For an expert who had lived to be one hundred, it was a simple matter.

When West had led a heart to trick three, East had failed to follow suit. Thus West was known to have started with six hearts originally. West had subsequently followed suit to three rounds of spades and three rounds of diamonds. Twelve of his thirteen cards were now accounted for.

When George later led a club to dummy's ace, West had played the six of clubs. And so all of West's thirteen cards were known—and the queen of clubs was not one of them. That card, therefore, had to be in the East hand.

I just hope that when I'm one hundred years old, I'll be able to think like that. As a matter of fact, when I get to be one hundred, I hope I'll be able to pick up thirteen cards and hold them.

• • •

Deal 7:

On this deal, declarer deliberately tossed a trick out of the window at trick one—and by so doing fulfilled a contract which was otherwise unmakable. I'd venture to guess that not one in a hundred of our nation's players would have made the winning play.

Both sides vulnerable. East dealer.

	North	
	♠ A 5 2 ♡ Q J 9 2 ◇ J 10 8 3 ♣ 10 6	
West		East
♠ 8 3 ♡ 6 4 ◇ 9 6 5 4 ♣ Q 9 8 5 3		♠ Q 10 9 7 4 ♡ A 8 5 ◇ A 7 ♣ K 7 2
	South	
	♠ K J 6 ♡ K 10 7 3 ◇ K Q 2 ♣ A J 4	

The bidding:

East	South	West	North
1 ♠	1 NT	Pass	2 NT
Pass	3 NT	Pass	Pass
Pass			

West elected to lead the five of clubs, East put up the king—and South paused before playing.

There was no doubt in South's mind that West had five, possibly six, clubs headed by the queen. With a lesser holding, surely West would have opened spades, East's bid suit. It was equally obvious that East, to have any semblance of an opening bid, had to have the two red aces.

Looking ahead, declarer perceived that if he captured the opening lead, he would have two club tricks. But if he did that and then led, say a heart, to drive out East's ace, then East would return a club, which the capable West defender would permit declarer to win. Then, when East obtained the lead with his diamond ace, he would play back his remaining club (assuming West held five clubs originally) and West would cash three club tricks. It therefore became imperative that the East-West communication in clubs be broken at once.

So declarer allowed West's king of clubs to win the opening lead. A club then came back, and declarer's jack was taken by West's queen. No matter what West now returned, declarer was home safely.

For the record, at trick three West shifted to a spade, which declarer won. It now became a routine proposition to drive out East's aces. All the defenders made were two club tricks and the two red aces.

• • •

Deal 8:

If it were possible to conduct a nationwide study to determine at what trick most game contracts are lost, I am sure that trick one would lead the other twelve by an overwhelming majority. The basic reason accounting for trick one's top position is that most bridgeplayers play too hurriedly to the first trick and do not look ahead to visualize the consequences of what might develop. And, inevitably, if the foundation is faulty, the superstructure must collapse.

As an illustration of the above, observe the following deal, which I use in my teaching to determine the degree of aptitude of pupils. The hand arose in a duplicate game in 1943, and was played by Richard Frey.

Neither side vulnerable. North dealer.

North

♠ A J 5
♡ 3 2
◇ 7 5
♣ A Q 10 9 6 3

West

♠ 10 9 8 6
♡ Q 10 6
◇ Q 10 8 4
♣ 7 2

East

♠ Q 7 4
♡ J 9 8 7
◇ J 9 2
♣ K J 5

South

♠ K 3 2
♡ A K 5 4
◇ A K 6 3
♣ 8 4

The bidding:

North	East	South	West
1 ♣	Pass	1 ♡	Pass
2 ♣	Pass	3 NT	Pass
Pass	Pass		

At virtually every table South arrived at a three-notrump contract. At four of these tables, the ten of spades was the opening lead. Yet, of the four South declarers, Frey was the only one who made an overtrick—the others all went down!

On the spade ten lead, Frey played dummy's five, East played the four, and South's king won. The eight of clubs was then led and the double finesse taken, losing to East's jack. A diamond was returned, South winning with the king, after which declarer's remaining club was played, the board's nine-spot being taken by East's king. Frey now had ten tricks: two spades, two hearts, two diamonds, and four clubs.

But look at the difference if the board's jack of spades is put up at trick one, in the hope that West is leading away from the queen. The jack is covered by the queen, and taken by declarer's king.* A club finesse is now tried, losing to East. Back comes a spade and dummy's ace of spades, the sole outside entry to dummy, is removed, thus making the to-be-established club suit uncashable.

From Frey's position, he perceived that he was going to attack the club suit in such a manner that if the finesse lost, it would lose only to East. By retaining dummy's A J of spades, he rendered it impossible for East to return a spade, except if East wanted to give declarer a present of a trick. Thus declarer, by not putting up the jack, obtained the timing (and the entry to dummy) essential to the establishment and cashing of the club suit.

Also, if declarer had the feeling that West possessed the queen of spades, he could finesse for that card later. But to have done so at trick one was needlessly dangerous—and, as it turned out, costly, as those who took the finesse discovered.

* If South declines to capture the queen, the ultimate result is not altered, for East returns a spade at trick two, putting South in the same position he would be in if he chose to win the queen at trick one.

Deal 9:

This deal arose in a ten-table duplicate game in 1944. Every South declarer arrived at a small slam contract in diamonds, but not one of them made it.* Yet, it was there for the taking!

East-West vulnerable. South dealer.

North

♠ Q J 10 9
♡ 9 5 3
♢ 5 2
♣ Q J 8 7

West

♠ A 6 3
♡ 7 4
♢ 8
♣ A K 10 9 6 4 2

East

♠ K 8 7 5 4 2
♡ J 10 8 6
♢ 10 6
♣ 3

South

♠ —
♡ A K Q 2
♢ A K Q J 9 7 4 3
♣ 5

The bidding (at one of the tables):

South	West	North	East
2 ♢	3 ♣	Double	Pass
4 NT	Pass	5 ♣	Pass
6 ♢	Pass	Pass	Pass

West opened the king of clubs, and switched to the spade ace at trick two, which South ruffed.

* Wartime bridge, perhaps?

To the nonexpert, the success of the contract would seem to depend on the six outstanding hearts being divided 3–3; or, on the remote possibility that one of the opponents possessed the doubleton J 10 of hearts. To the expert eye, another possibility would have suggested itself.

At trick three, a top trump would be led. Then would follow the ace, king, and queen of hearts, after which the fourth heart would be trumped with the board's remaining trump. And that would be it—a slam bid and made.

Admittedly, declarer would have been lucky to have found the defender with only two hearts with but a singleton trump. But what would it have cost declarer to avail himself of this possibility? It was "on the house": if two trumps were in the hand that possessed two hearts, the contract was unmakable.

• • •

Deal 10:

On this next deal, the bidding by South, an acknowledged-by-his-peers expert, left much to be desired. But the fact of the matter is that he was playing with a pupil in a duplicate game and our expert felt that if they could get a couple of good boards on this, the final round, they would win. So, rather than run the risk of having the pupil become the declarer—pupils learn to bid well before they learn to play well—our South expert "stole" the contract from his partner. The end result was most satisfactory, but the expert really had to sweat it out.

Neither side vulnerable. South dealer.

	North	
	♠ 8 3 ♡ K 10 9 8 6 ♢ A 7 5 2 ♣ J 2	
West ♠ J 10 9 6 4 ♡ 5 2 ♢ J 9 6 ♣ 7 6 4		**East** ♠ K Q 5 2 ♡ 7 4 3 ♢ Q 10 ♣ K 10 8 3
	South ♠ A 7 ♡ A Q J ♢ K 8 4 3 ♣ A Q 9 5	

South	West	North	East
1 ♢	Pass	1 ♡	Pass
2 NT	Pass	3 ♢	Pass
3 NT	Pass	Pass	Pass

Against the three-notrump contract, West opened the spade jack, and as soon as dummy came into view, South perceived that he was in an inferior contract: at three notrump there were just nine tricks, while at a four-heart contract ten tricks were guaranteed without breathing hard. So what good were nine tricks at notrump when ten tricks were available at hearts?

At the four-heart contract, the club finesse could be taken without any risk, after drawing trumps; if it lost, the opponents could cash just one spade trick. But if the club finesse lost at his three-notrump contract, the opponents would cash a bushel of spades. But, again, what good were nine tricks at notrump if everybody was making ten tricks at a heart contract?

The above were South's thoughts as he examined the combined hands. He concluded that caution and safety had to be thrown to the winds if he were to extricate himself and his partner. If he received a minus score for going down, it would be no worse than a plus score that figured to be worth nothing on a relative basis.

West's opening spade lead was permitted to win, after which another spade was played, East's queen being taken by declarer's ace. Five rounds of hearts were now taken, South discarding two diamonds from his own hand. East discarded his remaining spades, while West tossed two clubs and a spade.

With every intention of finessing in clubs for that vital overtrick, declarer next led the board's jack of clubs. Happily, East covered with the king and South's ace won. Ten tricks were now there for the taking.

But now another disquieting factor had entered onto the scene. With the favorable location of the club king being revealed, everybody who was in a four-heart contract would make at least eleven tricks, losing just a diamond and a spade (assuming the normal 3-2 division of the five outstanding diamonds). So South, if a good score were to be obtained, had to try for eleven tricks at his notrump contract.

The king and ace of diamonds were cashed next, after which the deuce of clubs was led off the board. When East followed with the eight-spot, South inserted his nine, with the prayer that East possessed the ten. As is evident, East had that key card, and the nine-spot captured the trick.

And so South wound up making eleven tricks: one spade, five hearts, two diamonds, and three clubs, for an excellent score, beating every other North-South pair but one. The only pair that outscored our expert was one that arrived at a six-heart contract, which was fulfilled by finessing twice in clubs (for the king and ten).

Deal 11:

We have all been in the position of wondering how to handle a trump suit consisting of A 9 facing the K J 10 x x x x. Should we play for the drop of the queen, or should we finesse? And if we finesse, which way to take it? With no clues to guide us, it became a pure guess—and on occasion we guessed right and on occasion we misguessed.

The following deal is concerned with the precise situation presented in the above paragraph. However, there was an external factor which influenced declarer's decision: it was the last deal of a duplicate game, and our declarer felt that he needed a top score on the board to stand a chance of winning. So he adopted a line of play which he thought might escape the other declarers, who, if they bid optimistically, would land in the identical contract. His reasoning in the play was expert, and he well deserved the handsome reward he received—a top score on the board.*

East-West vulnerable. North dealer.

North

♠ A 9
♡ K J 9 2
◇ J 5
♣ A 9 7 4 3

West

♠ Q 7 4
♡ 5 3
◇ 10 9 8 2
♣ Q 10 8 2

East

♠ 6
♡ Q 10 8 6
◇ A 7 6 4 3
♣ K J 5

South

♠ K J 10 8 5 3 2
♡ A 7 4
◇ K Q
♣ 6

* He and his partner, sad to relate, didn't win the game. They finished second, two points out of first place.

The bidding:

North	East	South	West
1 ♣	Pass	2 ♠	Pass
3 ♠	Pass	4 NT	Pass
5 ♡	Pass	6 ♠	Pass
Pass	Pass		

West opened the ten of diamonds, East taking his ace and returning a diamond, South's king winning.

As South now paused to survey the situation, it was apparent that the six-spade contract was not a happy one,* depending as it did on avoiding the loss of a spade trick *and* avoiding the loss of a heart trick. The first consideration was the trump suit—and there were no clues as to which opponent held the trump queen.

It being a fifty-fifty guess, declarer, after much thought, came up with something extra which he would have going for him *if* West held the trump queen. In this case—by finessing dummy's nine-spot—he would have two trump entries to dummy, giving him the opportunity of establishing the board's fifth club. If this could be accomplished, the necessity of the heart finesse would be eliminated, since declarer would then be enabled to discard his third heart on dummy's fifth club.

Having formulated his plan, declarer now proceeded to put it into action. At trick three he led his singleton club to dummy's ace, and ruffed a club with his ten-spot on the way back. A low trump was then led, and dummy's nine inserted, winning the trick. Another club was now led and ruffed, after which another trump was played to the board's ace, East discarding a diamond. With a prayer, a fourth lead of clubs was now made—and East discarded another diamond.

Declarer was now home, for West had just been revealed as the possessor of the outstanding club. South ruffed the fourth round of clubs, and laid down his king of spades, felling East's queen. He then entered dummy via the heart king, and on the fifth club discarded his losing heart.

As has been stated, a little skill *plus* a little (or more) luck can go a long way.

* The inferior six-spade contract that was arrived at was North's fault. Certainly, with his minimum hand, North should not have promptly raised South's two-spade jump response to three spades.

Deal 12:

The dividing line between the "good" and the "very good" duplicate player is a difficult one to delineate, for the players who comprise each of the two groups are all topnotch when it comes to basic skills: that is, to bidding and playing techniques, and to the application of deceptive tactics. But there unquestionably is a qualitative difference between the good and the very good, a difference that is often imperceptible to the objective observer, and which, when it does manifest itself, usually defies precise, black-on-white description.

It was my good fortune at a tournament some years ago to isolate a specific example of that ineffable "extra something" which is the predominant attribute of the "great" and the "very good." Permit me to introduce the situation as a problem in order that the reader can view it vicariously, as it confronted our very good player. The game was match-point duplicate.

North

♠ A K
♡ Q 10 6 5 3
♢ K 5 3 2
♣ 8 4

South

♠ 8 7
♡ A 4
♢ A J 8 6 4
♣ A J 9 2

You are sitting South, playing a *six-diamond* contract. West opens the king of clubs. What are your reactions as you gaze at the North-South cards? How do you feel about your contract? What are you going to do about it?

The average reaction probably would be: "How did I ever get to this silly, hopeless contract?" With this frame of mind firmly ingrained, the average declarer would now proceed to go down two tricks in average fashion, losing a diamond, a club, and a heart. The result, in match points, would be a "tie-for-bottom"—one-half a match point out of a possible twelve.

Our actual South declarer won the opening lead of the king of clubs with his ace, after which he plunked down the ace of hearts (there are days when singleton kings are floating around, but this was not one of them). Now came a diamond to dummy's king; then a finesse of the diamond jack was taken successfully. South now laid down the ace of diamonds, felling East's queen, and next led his remaining heart, West's king winning. West then cashed the queen of clubs, for the setting trick.

And just what, you may properly ask, is so good (let alone "very good") about going down one at a slam contract? Well, I agree that you'll win no tournaments if it develops into a habit. However, to continue, after South had gone down a trick he examined the East-West cards and remarked: "Not too bad. Probably at least an average board."

Now, gentle reader, may I ask for your opinion? Why should being down one to an overbid slam contract, which the field didn't figure to arrive at, become at least an average board—and how did our declarer sense that it was? For the record, North-South received seven match points out of twelve for being down one!

Let's take a look at all four hands:

North

♠ A K
♡ Q 10 6 5 3
◇ K 5 3 2
♣ 8 4

West

♠ J 10 9 3 2
♡ K J 7 2
◇ 9
♣ K Q 3

East

♠ Q 6 5 4
♡ 9 8
◇ Q 10 7
♣ 10 7 6 5

South

♠ 8 7
♡ A 4
◇ A J 8 6 4
♣ A J 9 2

When our South declarer originally surveyed the North-South hands, he came to the conclusion that three notrump figured to be the normal contract. Against the probable spade opening—from either side, since spades had not been bid, and the opponents had more spades than any other suit—declarer would have to bring in *five* diamond tricks (or, instead, if he were real lucky, *four* heart tricks) to fulfill his contract. Knowing from past experiences that the field would play the king and ace of diamonds to drop the queen—as opposed to finessing the jack—our declarer realized that if the queen wouldn't drop, then three notrump figured to go down a trick, or more. Consequently he finessed for the diamond queen, hoping that the adverse diamonds were divided 3–1. Only if they were so divided could he hope to tie with those who would be going down at three notrump. If the diamonds were divided 2–2, then the entire North-South field would be making at least three notrump—and no matter how the adverse diamonds happened to be divided, he would always be defeated at his slam contract.

A simple hand? In retrospect only, if at all. The mere "good" player, observing the North-South hands at a six-diamond contract, would undoubtedly succumb to the enticing delusion of normal optimism: to the highly remote chance that one of the opponents was dealt the singleton king of hearts. And when this possibility failed to materialize, hope would vanish forever and inertia would set in. He would then follow through with the motions, play the king and ace of diamonds from force of habit, and go down two tricks.

But our "very good" expert—shall we say "great"?—would adopt a different approach when the heart king failed to drop. Recognizing all along that he was in a doomed contract, his primary thought would be centered around how he could best extricate himself with the minimum loss. And, as the reader has witnessed, seven match points out of twelve was a pretty good salvage job—so good, as a matter of fact, that it enabled North-South to win the event by three match points.

chapter 11

WELL-PLAYED AND WELL-DEFENDED HANDS

In each of the deals featured in this chapter, there is presented a fleeting moment in the bridge life of the topflight expert: a hand played magnificently; an inspired defensive play; or a highly imaginative analysis of a situation which led to the defeat of his adversary.

Deal 1:

At a small-slam contract in rubber bridge, declarer never tries for an overtrick if, in so trying, he jeopardizes his contract. And, conversely, when defending against a small-slam contract in rubber bridge, the defenders always exert a maximum all-out effort to defeat that contract, even if in so trying they present declarer with an insignificant overtrick.

In this deal, which occurred in a New York tournament some years ago, our South declarer, Claggett Bowie of Baltimore, reached an easily-makable small-slam contract. Claggett knew his West opponent to be a good rubber-bridge player who had but recently started to play duplicate bridge. Capitalizing on this knowledge, Claggett was able to bring home an "unmakable" overtrick—without jeopardizing his contract. It is my belief that very few of our topflight players would have made that all-important (in duplicate) overtrick.

Here is the deal:

Neither side vulnerable. South dealer.

North

♠ A Q 9 7 4
♡ J 5 3
◊ A J
♣ A 10 5

West

♠ 8 6 3
♡ K 9
◊ 10 7 4 3 2
♣ J 8 7

East

♠ —
♡ 10 8 7 6 4
◊ 9 8 6 5
♣ 9 6 3 2

South

♠ K J 10 5 2
♡ A Q 2
◊ K Q
♣ K Q 4

The bidding:

South	West	North	East
1 ♠	Pass	3 ♣	Pass
4 ♣	Pass	4 ◊	Pass
4 ♡	Pass	5 ♠	Pass
6 ♠	Pass	Pass	Pass

When the dummy came into view, it was apparent to Bowie that twelve tricks were there for the taking. Had this deal arisen in a rubber-bridge game, Claggett could have relaxed. But not only was this a duplicate game, where an overtrick is always of vital importance, but also it was obvious that twelve tricks could be made at six notrump; and, assuredly, at least a few North-South pairs figured to arrive at the latter contract, scoring 990 points against Claggett's six-spade contract, which would score "only" 980 points. However, an overtrick at the six-spade contract would give Claggett a score of 1010 points.

West's opening lead was the three of spades, upon which East discarded the four of hearts as South's five-spot won the trick. The king and ace of trumps were cashed next, picking up the adverse pieces of trump.

The extra trick, if it were to be made, had to come from the heart suit. One of the possibilities for this to be accomplished would be if East had been dealt the doubleton king of hearts. In this case, the successful finesse of the queen, followed by the cashing of the heart ace, would fell East's king, resulting in dummy's jack being promoted into a winner. But this possibility was just about nil, based on East's discard of a low heart at trick one: if East had held exactly the K x x of hearts, he surely would have made some discard other than a low heart at trick one. Another possibility—theoretical—was for West to have been dealt the singleton king of hearts. This was a most remote possibility, mathematically speaking.

After due deliberation, Claggett came up with an inspirational solution. As was mentioned in passing a few paragraphs back, his solution was based on the knowledge that West was a good rubber-bridge player; and, as such, it was instinctive for him to think first about setting the slam contract rather than to prevent an overtrick from being made.

After drawing trumps, Bowie cashed his two top diamonds, and his three top clubs. He then laid down his ace of hearts—and prayed!

West knew that South had started with three hearts (West had counted South for five spades, three clubs, and two diamonds), and it was his hope that South had the A x x of hearts. He perceived that if he won the second heart lead with the king, he would have no option but to lead a diamond, which would enable South to ruff in dummy while simultaneously discarding his last losing heart from his own hand.

So, logically (rubber-bridge speaking), West tossed his king of hearts on Bowie's lead of the ace, with the fervent hope that East held the Q 10 x of hearts, and would thereby be enabled to win two heart tricks after South's second heart lead. As it turned out however, Bowie was now able to claim the rest of the tricks.

In conclusion, West's jettisoning of the heart king would have been the only correct play at rubber bridge. But, at duplicate, could West have been that clairvoyant to have known that declarer was playing for an overtrick, and not for his contract?

Deal 2:

At times, in duplicate, if one is to obtain a good score, he must gamble for an overtrick at the risk of losing his contract. On this deal, however, there was no really legitimate chance for declarer to make an overtrick, but there was a good possibility that his left-hand opponent might slip. As it turned out, declarer's judgment in taking a gamble was vindicated (if one judges by results), and the overtrick gave him a top score on the board.

Neither side vulnerable. South dealer.

North

♠ 10 2
♡ A 9 4 3
♢ A Q 10 9
♣ 7 4 3

West

♠ J 9 7 5
♡ Q 6
♢ 4 3
♣ A 10 8 6 2

East

♠ 8 6 3
♡ K J 10 5
♢ 8 7 5 2
♣ J 9

South

♠ A K Q 4
♡ 8 7 2
♢ K J 6
♣ K Q 5

The bidding:

South	West	North	East
1 NT	Pass	3 NT	Pass
Pass	Pass		

West made the normal opening lead of the six of clubs and East's jack fell to declarer's queen. Declarer had just fulfilled his contract —that is, it was there for the taking. But, in duplicate bridge, fulfilling a game contract is not necessarily a guarantee of victory. So declarer gave thoughts to making an overtrick.

It was, of course, obvious to declarer that West held the club ace, for if East had held that card, he would have played it. Any hope of making a second club winner on his own power was thus an impossibility.

As declarer viewed the setup, there was a fifty-fifty chance that West held the spade jack. If such were the case, then an immediate lead of the spade four toward dummy's ten might make a winner out of the ten-spot. This reasoning was based on the realization that West, holding the J x x x or J x x, would probably play low on the spade lead, trusting that East would be able to win the trick and return a club to entrap declarer's king. (It was apparent to West that declarer held the club king, for if East had held that card, he would have played it at trick one.)

Having the courage of his convictions, declarer led the spade four at trick two—and West played the five! The board's ten of spades was put up, and it won the trick. Declarer had successfully walked a tightrope.

Had West taken his jack of spades at trick two, declarer would not have lost anything, as his remaining K 5 of clubs would have effectively prevented West from cashing his suit. And, if East had possessed the spade jack, declarer would still have had a reasonable chance of fulfilling his contract, which would in this case have depended on the adversely held seven clubs being divided 4–3 or 6–1.

Actually, the only setup that would have resulted in the defeat of declarer's contract would have been if the outstanding clubs were divided 5–2 *and* if East also held the spade jack.

Deal 3:

There are times in bridge when it is apparent that one has no control over one's destiny. In such circumstances the true expert—a topflight technician at all times—is often able to force his adversaries into making a mistake, and thereby gain him the victory that he could never have made on his own power. Here is an illustration. The deal was played in a duplicate game in 1943.

Both sides vulnerable. South dealer.

North

♠ A 10 6 4
♡ A Q 9 5
◇ 8 6 3
♣ 7 4

West

♠ 8 7 5
♡ 6 3 2
◇ 10 9
♣ K J 9 3 2

East

♠ K J 2
♡ 7 4
◇ K J 7 4
♣ Q 10 8 5

South

♠ Q 9 3
♡ K J 10 8
◇ A Q 5 2
♣ A 6

The bidding:

South	West	North	East
1 NT	Pass	3 NT	Pass
Pass	Pass		

When West opened the three of clubs against South's three-notrump contract, the latter perceived that he had just seven top tricks; and that even with a successful diamond finesse, he would end up one trick short of his contract. And, of course, if he attacked the spade suit to try for his ninth trick, the opponents would obtain the lead and cash sufficient clubs to beat him. His only chance, he reasoned, lay in the hope that the opponents, if given the opportunity, might slip.

South won the opening club lead and promptly led back a club! West won with the nine, and then proceeded to cash the king of clubs and the jack of clubs. This was the position just prior to West's cashing of his last club, the deuce:

	North	
	♠ A 10 6 ♡ A Q 9 5 ◊ 8 6 ♣ —	
West		East
♠ 8 7 5 ♡ 6 3 2 ◊ 10 9 ♣ 2		♠ K J 2 ♡ 7 4 ◊ K J 7 4 ♣ —
	South	
	♠ Q 9 ♡ K J 10 8 ◊ A Q 5 ♣ —	

To trick five, West now led the deuce of clubs, dummy discarded the spade six, East signaled violently with the spade jack, and declarer tossed his eight of hearts. West, quite naturally, shifted to the spade eight, and declarer climbed up with dummy's ace, knowing that East possessed the spade king. Declarer now proceeded to run dummy's four heart tricks, arriving at this position before leading the board's final heart:

	North	
	♠ 10 ♡ A ♢ 8 6 ♣ —	
West		**East**
♠ 7 5 ♡ — ♢ 10 9 ♣ —		♠ K ♡ — ♢ K J 7 ♣ —
	South	
	♠ Q ♡ — ♢ A Q 5 ♣ —	

To trick ten, dummy's ace of hearts was led, and East found himself caught in a squeeze: if he discarded the spade king, declarer's queen would become a winner. And if, instead, he tossed away the seven of diamonds, he would promote South's five-spot into a winning trick.

Actually—and properly—East elected to discard the diamond seven, hoping his partner held the queen. Declarer, of course, discarded his spade queen. A diamond was now led off dummy, East followed with the jack, and declarer successfully finessed his queen. Then followed the ace of diamonds, dropping East's king. The five of diamonds had just become declarer's game-going trick.

In a broad sense, we might say that South squeezed East. In a more precise sense, the fact is that West squeezed his partner by cashing the fifth club, thereby putting his partner into a squeeze position at trick ten.

Had West not cashed the fifth club, declarer might have made his contract by establishing a spade trick—but, then again, he might not have. It would depend on how he played the spades.

But the point of this deal is not what might have been. It is this question: who but an imaginative expert, thoroughly familiar with the application of squeezes and endplays, would have won the opening lead and shot back a club, thus giving the opponents the opportunity of going wrong?

A concluding word, to those who think that West might have cashed five club tricks (in theory). It couldn't be, for West had opened the three-spot as his fourth-highest, which meant that he couldn't possibly have started with more than five clubs. Nor could East have possessed more than five clubs. Thus, declarer's play was "safe"—at least to the extent of not being defeated immediately.

• • •

Deal 4:

As *declarer,* has it ever made any difference to you whenever you held the 10 9 8 of a suit, whether you led the eight, the nine, or the ten? Think back. I'll wager you can't recall one instance in which the card you played affected the outcome.

In the 1930's, a deal was played in which had declarer led the ten, he would have failed to fulfill his slam contract. This is it.

East-West vulnerable. North dealer.

North
♠ 7 6 2
♡ A Q 9
◊ Q J 9 7 3
♣ Q 5

West
♠ 10 9 5
♡ K 10 8 6 5 3
◊ K 8
♣ J 7

East
♠ J 3
♡ J 7 4 2
◊ 10 6 4 2
♣ K 6 2

South
♠ A K Q 8 4
♡ —
◊ A 5
♣ A 10 9 8 4 3

The bidding:

North	East	South	West
Pass	Pass	1 ♠	Pass
2 ◊	Pass	4 ♣	Pass
4 ♠	Pass	5 ♣	Pass
5 ♡	Pass	6 ♠*	Pass
Pass	Pass		

* An overbid, justified only by the result.

West opened the ten of spades which was taken by declarer's king. Declarer now made the psychological play of the *eight* of clubs. His reason, as he put it, was: "If West held the king of clubs, he would have to go up no matter what I played, whereas if he held the jack, he would probably play low on the eight, but would probably cover the ten, destroying dummy's only entry, the queen of clubs."

As South had hoped, West played the seven of clubs on the eight, the five-spot was played from dummy, and East was compelled to win the trick with his king. East shifted to a diamond, and declarer promptly put up his ace. He then led a club to the queen, after which he discarded his losing diamond on the board's ace of hearts. Trumps were now drawn, and declarer claimed the balance of the tricks.

How different the result would have been if, at trick two, declarer had led the *ten* of clubs. West would have covered with the jack, and dummy's queen would have been taken by East's king. When a diamond would now come back, there would be no way for declarer to avoid the loss of a diamond trick, for he could never reach dummy to take his discard on the ace of hearts.

Of course, if West had covered the eight of clubs (at trick two) with the jack, the slam contract would have been defeated. But could any mortal have been that clairvoyant?

• • •

Deal 5:

A complaint occasionally heard in amateur circles is, "Partner, that was *my* ace you trumped!" The usual apology is, "Partner, I didn't know it was your ace. I thought it was *his* (or her) ace."

Here is a 1943 deal that concerns itself with the trumping of partner's ace by design, and not through ignorance. The deal arose in a rubber-bridge game, and not in a tournament, and is being introduced as a change of pace. However, had it taken place in a duplicate game, I'm certain that the identical play would have been made.

North-South vulnerable. West dealer.

North

♠ A K J 10
♡ Q J
◇ A K Q 2
♣ 6 5 3

West

♠ 2
♡ A K 10 9 5 3
◇ 10 7 4
♣ A Q 8

East

♠ 7 6 4
♡ 4
◇ J 9 6 5 3
♣ 10 9 7 2

South

♠ Q 9 8 5 3
♡ 8 7 6 2
◇ 8
♣ K J 4

The bidding:

West	North	East	South
1 ♡	Double	Pass	1 ♠
2 ♡	2 ♠	Pass	3 ♠
Pass	4 ♠	Pass	Pass
Pass			

Sitting West was Al Sobel, currently the chief director of the American Contract Bridge League. His partner, sitting East, was his wife, Helen Sobel.

West opened the king of hearts, and followed up with the ace. It was rather obvious that the defenders couldn't make more than a total of two heart tricks, and could make no spades and no diamonds. It was equally apparent that if West's ace of hearts were permitted to win the second trick, a third heart lead would be ruffed in dummy with a high trump. Diamonds offered no hope for the defenders. So, by elimination, if the defense had any chance of defeating the four-spade contract, the club suit had to be attacked at once.

So Mrs. Sobel trumped her partner's ace of hearts at trick two and laid down the ten of clubs. West now made two club tricks. Had the ace of hearts not been trumped, South would easily have fulfilled the contract.

After West cashed the setting trick in clubs, South exposed his hand, claiming, "The rest are mine."

Al Sobel then turned to Helen and gasped, "Partner, you trumped my ace! . . . THANKS."

• • •

Deal 6:

One of the most aggravating situations in bridge arises when the opponents reach a slam and your choices of leads are dangerous ones. Possibly recalling a similar situation where the dangerous lead proved costly, you lead a trump, as a "neutral," "safe" lead. At times, the trump lead is successful; and, at times, the dangerous lead would have been the winning one.

Here is a deal that presented such a problem when it arose in a tournament in 1942.

Neither side vulnerable. South dealer.

North

♠ A 9 4 3
♡ A Q J 6 5 2
◇ 8
♣ 7 5

West

♠ 6 5
♡ K 10 8
◇ K 9 5 4
♣ K 9 6 3

East

♠ Q J 7
♡ 9 4 3
◇ J 10 7 2
♣ Q 10 2

South

♠ K 10 8 2
♡ 7
◇ A Q 6 3
♣ A J 8 4

The bidding:

South	West	North	East
1 ◇	Pass	1 ♡	Pass
1 ♠	Pass	3 ♡	Pass
3 NT	Pass	4 ♠	Pass
6 ♠	Pass	Pass	Pass

If West makes the safe lead of a trump, declarer will probably fulfill his contract. He will win East's jack with the king, finesse the jack of hearts, cash the heart ace (discarding a club), and ruff a heart, thus establishing the suit.

Then will come a trump to the ace, leaving the queen outstanding. Hearts will now be run, and all the defenders can make is the high trump.

From the West seat, North's bidding indicates that he has an excellent heart suit. As West looks at his K 10 8 of hearts, he should know that declarer will bring home dummy's hearts, either by finessing or by ruffing a couple of dummy's hearts. Hence, based on the bidding, a passive trump lead figures to be costly. And, since South has opened the bidding with one diamond, the aggressive lead of a club appears to be West's best hope.

At the table, when the deal was actually encountered, West did open a low club, and East's queen fell to declarer's ace. There was now no way of preventing the defenders from making one club trick and one trump trick.

• • •

Deal 7:

The next deal arose some twenty-five years ago, and it illustrates how important the play at trick one can be. The South declarer was the late Geoffrey Mott-Smith.

North-South vulnerable. South dealer.

North

♠ 8 6
♡ A K 6
◇ Q 9 7
♣ A 10 9 8 4

West

♠ A Q 10 5 3
♡ Q J 10 7 3
◇ 4
♣ J 5

East

♠ J 9 2
♡ 9 8 4 2
◇ 6 3 2
♣ K Q 2

South

♠ K 7 4
♡ 5
◇ A K J 10 8 5
♣ 7 6 3

The bidding:

South	West	North	East
1 ◇	1 ♠	2 ♣	Pass
2 ◇	2 ♡	3 ♡	Pass
3 NT	4 ♡	5 ◇	Pass
Pass	Pass		

The bidding was typical, aggressive, match-point style, especially by a nonvulnerable West.*

The opening lead was the heart queen—and if Mott-Smith had made the normal and natural play of winning the trick, he would have gone down! Had he won the trick, then when East obtained the lead with a club, a spade shift would have given West two tricks in that suit.

But declarer foresaw this eventuality—and he permitted the queen of hearts to win the opening lead! West now led the club jack, dummy's ace winning. On the ace and king of hearts, declarer discarded his two remaining clubs.

A club was then ruffed high in the closed hand, after which the diamond five was led to the board's seven-spot. Another club was now ruffed high, and the club suit had become established. A trump was next led to the board's nine, and the queen of trumps then played, picking up East's last trump. On the two high clubs in dummy, declarer discarded two of his spades. At the end, West made his ace of spades.

• • •

* West would have gone down but one trick at his four-heart contract.

Deal 8:

When one is born into the world of bridge, the first thing one learns is to extract the opponents' trumps at the first opportunity. The application of this philosophy usually pays handsome dividends—but not always.

Here is a deal where if the adverse trumps were drawn immediately, declarer would have gone down. It is really a simple hand, but I imagine that many of our nation's nonexpert bridgeplayers would have flubbed it. The South declarer was John C. Stablein of Seattle, Washington.

Both sides vulnerable. South dealer.

North
♠ 8 4
♡ K Q 9 2
♢ K 6 4
♣ 10 8 6 4

West
♠ 6 3
♡ A 7 4 3
♢ Q J 10 5
♣ A 7 2

East
♠ 10 7 2
♡ J 10 6
♢ 9 7 2
♣ Q J 9 3

South
♠ A K Q J 9 5
♡ 8 5
♢ A 8 3
♣ K 5

The bidding:

South	West	North	East
1 ♠	Pass	1 NT	Pass
4 ♠	Pass	Pass	Pass

The queen of diamonds was opened, Mr. Stablein taking the trick with his ace. He then cashed the ace of trumps—and stopped playing trumps. He now led a heart, West followed with a low one, and dummy's king won. The board's remaining trump was next played to declarer's king, after which East's last trump was picked up.

South's last heart was now led, West taking his ace. On dummy's queen of hearts declarer later discarded his losing diamond. Eventually, he lost two club tricks.

Had declarer drawn trumps immediately, then when he led a heart, dummy's king would have won, as it did. But now declarer would have been unable to return to his own hand to lead another heart toward dummy's queen. The result would then have been that he would have lost a heart, two clubs, *and* a diamond.

Mr. Stablein, of course, foresaw this problem of "entries"—and, hence, led just one round of trumps. He was thus enabled to utilize the board's second trump as a reentry back to the closed hand.

• • •

Deal 9:

The next deal contains nothing brilliant or spectacular. But it does serve as a typical example of the simple, logical, looking-ahead approach which is inherent in the expert's mature makeup.

East-West vulnerable. South dealer.

North

♠ J 5 3
♡ A 6 5
◇ A J 9 7 3
♣ 9 4

West

♠ 6
♡ Q J 10 8
◇ 10 8 5 2
♣ Q 10 8 6

East

♠ K 7 4 2
♡ K 4
◇ 4
♣ A J 7 5 3 2

South

♠ A Q 10 9 8
♡ 9 7 3 2
◇ K Q 6
♣ K

The bidding:

South	West	North	East
1 ♠	Pass	2 ◇	Pass
2 ♠	Pass	3 ♠	Pass
4 ♠	Pass	Pass	Pass

Sitting in the South seat was the late Olive Peterson, one of the world's finest women players and the winner of numerous national championships.

West made the normal opening lead of the heart queen, which was won by dummy's ace as East unblocked with the king of hearts (so that the way would be clear for West to cash hearts when either East or West regained the lead).

At trick two, Olive led dummy's jack of spades, and took a successful finesse against East's king. Another spade finesse then followed, declarer's queen being inserted. West discarded the six of clubs.

I could be wrong, but I imagine that many of our players, had they been sitting South, would now have led a low diamond to the board's jack in order to take a third spade finesse. Had this been done, then when the king of diamonds would subsequently have been led, it would have been revealed that West had started with the 10 x x x of diamonds. There would now be no way to bring home dummy's diamond suit, since to overtake the queen with the ace (on the third lead of the suit) would promote West's ten-spot into a winner.

But Olive foresaw that if the five adversely held diamonds were divided 3–2, then it would cost nothing to overtake the king with the ace right now (trick four) in order to reenter the dummy: and if they were divided 4–1 instead, then West might well have started with the 10 x x x of diamonds.

So, at trick four, she led her king of diamonds, and overtook it with dummy's ace. The board's last trump was then played, and another successful finesse was taken against East's king of trumps, after which South's trump ace felled East's king.

The queen of diamonds was cashed next, East discarding a club. Now declarer's six of diamonds was led, West followed with the eight, and dummy's nine was inserted, with the guarantee that it would win.

On the jack and seven of diamonds, Olive discarded two of her heart losers. Thus she made an overtrick at her four-spade contract, an overtrick that was worth its weight in gold, for only two other declarers made eleven tricks at the four-spade contract. The result was a three-way tie for top on the deal, with Olive's name being one of those whose names led all the rest.

Deal 10:

One of the world's topflight players—women and *men* included—is Edith Kemp of Miami Beach, Florida. Here is an example of the functioning of her mind. The deal arose in a team-of-four match. Edith was South.

Neither side vulnerable. South dealer.

North

♠ J 9
♡ Q 7 5 2
◇ Q J 9 3 2
♣ A J

West

♠ K 5 4
♡ A 10 6
◇ 10 8
♣ 10 7 6 3 2

East

♠ 10 8 7 6 3 2
♡ J 4 3
◇ 7
♣ K 5 4

South

♠ A Q
♡ K 9 8
◇ A K 6 5 4
♣ Q 9 8

The bidding:

South	West	North	East
1 ◇	Pass	1 ♡	Pass
2 NT	Pass	3 NT	Pass
Pass	Pass		

West opened the three of clubs and Edith stopped to analyze the situation when dummy came into view. This was the way she reasoned: "If I take the club finesse and it loses, a spade return by East might defeat my contract.* But if I go up with the ace of clubs, I can almost surely bring in nine tricks by setting up a heart, or possibly two heart tricks. And if I can't get two heart tricks, I should have the time to build up a second club trick."

So up South went with the board's ace of clubs and ran five diamond tricks, ending up in dummy. She then led the deuce of hearts and, as she put it: "If East had held the ace of hearts and played it, I would have my nine tricks: five diamonds, a spade, a club, and two hearts. And if East didn't play it, my heart king would win the trick, after which I would promote my queen of clubs into my ninth trick." †

When the deuce of hearts was led off dummy, East played the three, and South's king was taken by West's ace. If West now led either a spade or a club, he would establish a ninth trick for declarer. And if he chose to return a heart instead, declarer would put up dummy's queen, after which she would concede the jack of clubs to the king, thus creating her own ninth trick.

At the table, West, upon winning the heart ace, led a club, and declarer had made her contract.

Edith's comment after the session was: "When the scores were posted, nine South declarers arrived at three notrump. Only three of us made it." ‡

• • •

* She was right! A spade lead by East at trick two would have established East's spade suit.

† By leading a low club to the dummy's jack.

‡ I'll wager the other six played it differently.

Deal 11:

As has been demonstrated in earlier illustrations, one of the qualities that enables the expert to rise above his fellow bridgeplayers is his ability, in apparently dire circumstances, to "create" the condition that must exist if he is to survive. And, having created the condition, he then proceeds on the assumption that it is a reality. Here is an example, taken from a team-of-four match in 1932. Sitting South was George Unger of New York City.

Both sides vulnerable. South dealer.

North

♠ 10 8
♡ 6 4 3
♢ 9 7 5 2
♣ 8 6 4 3

West

♠ 9 7 6
♡ 9 8 5 2
♢ K Q 4
♣ Q J 10

East

♠ 4 2
♡ K 10 7
♢ J 10 8
♣ A K 9 7 2

South

♠ A K Q J 5 3
♡ A Q J
♢ A 6 3
♣ 5

The bidding:

South	West	North	East
2 ♠	Pass	2 NT	Pass
3 ♠	Pass	3 NT	Pass
4 ♠	Pass	Pass	Pass

West opened the queen of clubs, which held the trick, after which he continued with the club jack. West overtook with his king —and South did not play for forty-five seconds while he studied the setup. These were his reflections: "The loss of two diamonds is inevitable. If I am to fulfill my contract, I must bring home the queen and jack of hearts. Unfortunately, I have only one sure entry to dummy, and thus can't take two heart finesses.

"However, if West has the nine of trumps, I can get to the board a second time by finessing dummy's eight-spot. And East had better have the king of hearts—if he doesn't, I'm done for."

Having thus reasoned, George trumped the second club lead with his jack (preserving the three and five as entry cards to dummy), and then led the trump three. West followed suit with the six, and George, with his heart in his mouth, inserted the board's eight-spot. When East played the deuce on this trick, George was halfway home.

A heart was now led, and the finesse of the queen taken—successfully. Dummy was reentered via the spade ten, and the finesse in hearts was repeated, declarer's jack winning. The ace of spades was next laid down, picking up West's last trump. At the end, George gave away two diamond tricks—and was quite pleased by the outcome: game in spades bid and made.

The moral? Simple. A little luck plus a little imagination plus a little skill can take you a long way.

• • •

Deal 12:

The joint themes of this deal are falsecarding by a declarer and signaling by a defender, subjects which are of vital importance in the daily lives of all bridgeplayers. The deal arose in a duplicate game at the Toronto Whist Club in 1933.

Both sides vulnerable. West dealer.

North

♠ J 5 4
♡ A K J 8
◇ Q 8 6
♣ A Q 3

West

♠ A
♡ 10 6 2
◇ A K 10 9 5 4
♣ J 10 9

East

♠ 7 2
♡ Q 9 5 3
◇ 3
♣ K 8 7 5 4 2

South

♠ K Q 10 9 8 6 3
♡ 7 4
◇ J 7 2
♣ 6

The bidding:

West	North	East	South
1 ◇	1 NT	Pass	4 ♠
Pass	Pass	Pass	

At virtually every table South arrived at a four-spade contract, against which West opened the king of diamonds. Some of the declarers got real "cute" and falsecarded with the diamond jack. Where the West defenders were observant, they perceived the "unappearance" of the diamond deuce, and continued with the ace of diamonds, East discarding a club. A third diamond was then ruffed by East and eventually West made his ace of trumps for the setting trick.

At one of the tables each of the participants was an expert. Sitting East was John W. Jacobson, one of Canada's top players. The bidding given in the diagram occurred at this table.

West opened the king of diamonds and declarer played the deuce, not the jack or seven. From West's position, the deuce might well have been a singleton, and a continuation of the diamond ace might result in the establishment of dummy's queen as declarer trumped. Logically, West shifted to the jack of clubs, and dummy's ace was put up. On this trick Mr. Jacobson, East, did not play the card most nonexpert players would have played, namely the eight as a "come-on" signal. He followed suit with the deuce of clubs: "No interest, partner."

Declarer now led dummy's jack of spades, West's ace winning. Perceiving the hopelessness of continuing clubs, and seeing no future in hearts, what was there to do but to lay down the diamond ace? When East discarded a club on this trick, West hurriedly led another diamond for East to trump.

And thus the consequence of good declarer's play, and intelligent reasoning on the part of the defenders, brought about the "par" result: four spades was down one.

• • •

Deal 13:

This deal arose in a tournament in the late thirties. Its story is presented in two parts. The first analysis illustrates what happened at one table, where an expert South declarer was playing against a nonexpert East defender. The second narrative describes the happenings when the deal was replayed with an expert South declarer pitted against an equally expert East defender.

East-West vulnerable. South dealer.

North

♠ A K 10
♡ A K 8 3
♢ 7 5 4 2
♣ 8 4

West

♠ 7 6
♡ 6 4
♢ J 10 8
♣ K J 9 5 3 2

East

♠ 9 8 5 3 2
♡ Q J 10 9
♢ K 9
♣ Q 10

South

♠ Q J 4
♡ 7 5 2
♢ A Q 6 3
♣ A 7 6

The bidding:

South	West	North	East
1 ♢	Pass	1 ♡	Pass
1 NT	Pass	3 NT	Pass
Pass	Pass		

At both tables, the above-described bidding took place. The two final results, however, were quite different.

1. Expert South Declarer versus Nonexpert East Defender

West opened the five of clubs, and East's queen was permitted to win the trick. East returned the ten of clubs, which West overtook with the jack when South played low. For lack of a better return, West played back the king of clubs, South's ace winning as dummy discarded a diamond and East tossed away a spade.

Our declarer now analyzed the situation thusly: "I have just seven tricks, and even if I can create another by establishing dummy's fourth heart, I'll still have to attack the diamond suit to make my game-going trick. So why bother with the hearts—I'll pin my hopes on getting two more diamond tricks. . . . Of course, if West ever gets the lead, I'll be done for."

At trick four, declarer led a spade to dummy's ace, after which a low diamond was led, declarer successfully finessing his queen. If he had now played the ace and another diamond, he would have gone down, since *West* would have won the third diamond lead with his jack.

But declarer, knowing that his self-preservation depended on West being kept out of the lead, didn't bang down the diamond ace. Instead, he reentered dummy via a spade, and led a second diamond off dummy. East perforce played the king, South heaved a sigh of relief—and, of course, allowed the king to win the trick. No matter what East now returned (actually, he chose the heart queen), declarer had his contracted-for nine tricks: three spades, two hearts, three diamonds, and one club.

2. Expert South Declarer versus Equally Expert East Defender

At this table, the defense started along the same path: West led the five of clubs, and declarer declined to take East's queen. When East came back with the club ten, West again overtook with his jack and returned the club king, declarer winning with his ace. On this trick, a diamond was discarded from dummy—and East thought for quite a while before he made his discard. These were his thoughts:

"My partner's club suit is established, but how can he ever get the lead to cash the suit? Certainly not in either spades or hearts, that's obvious. So it's got to be in the diamond suit—or nowhere.

"If my partner has either the ace or queen of diamonds, we're in good shape; and if declarer has both of these cards, then without a doubt my king is hopelessly trapped, with no escape, for declarer, if he needs it, will take a successful finesse against my king. My king is really quite useless to me—but if I can get it out of the way, then perhaps I can create a reentry for my partner."

And so it came to pass that when West led the king of clubs to trick three, East did not toss away his useless spade (as was done at the other table). Instead he discarded his "useless" *king of diamonds!*

Declarer was now unable to fulfill his contract, for he couldn't establish another diamond winner without permitting West to regain the lead. Fully appreciative of his position, South led a low heart out of his hand at trick four, and inserted the board's eight-spot, passing the lead to the nondangerous East hand. His hope was, of course, that the six outstanding hearts were divided 3–3 in which case dummy's fourth heart would be promoted into a winner. As can be evidenced, they weren't so divided, and eventually declarer was forced to concede his defeat.

• • •

Deal 14:

On this hand there is no hero and there is no goat. The deal illustrates excellent defenders' thinking and declarer's thinking, with the ultimate victory going to the declarer. This hand, incidentally, also gives a graphic picture of the bidding fight for the part-score which is inherent in duplicate bridge.

North-South vulnerable. North dealer.

North

♠ 4 3 2
♡ J 5 3
◇ 10 7
♣ A Q 10 6 5

West

♠ K 8
♡ A K 10 8 6
◇ 8 6
♣ K 7 3 2

East

♠ 9 5
♡ Q 7 4
◇ A Q 9 5 3
♣ 9 8 4

South

♠ A Q J 10 7 6
♡ 9 2
◇ K J 4 2
♣ J

The bidding:

North	East	South	West
Pass	Pass	1 ♠	2 ♡
Pass	Pass	2 ♠	Pass
Pass	3 ♡	Pass	Pass
3 ♠	Double	Pass	Pass
Pass			

East's double, by the way, was a typical match-point gambling bid, made with the hope of setting South one trick, for a score of 200. This score of 200, when neither side can make a game, will usually give the recipient a top score on the board. (Had the game been rubber bridge, East would not have dreamed of doubling.)

The king of hearts was opened, East playing the seven-spot, after which the ace of hearts was led, East following with the four. Since East had raised hearts, it was apparent to West that East's "high-low" signal for a heart continuation showed possession of the queen rather than a doubleton. West, therefore, knew that South would ruff a third heart lead. At trick three, West shifted to the three of clubs, hoping that he could talk declarer out of taking a club finesse.

South climbed right up with dummy's ace, not because he was afraid to take the finesse, but rather because he felt he had no particular need for one discard from his own hand *if* the club finesse happened to succeed. He then led a diamond, East putting up the ace, after which East returned the heart queen, South ruffing.

Declarer next led the king of diamonds, and he followed up with another diamond, intending to ruff it in dummy. But West spiked this plan by ruffing the diamond with his eight of trumps (dummy discarding a club).

West now had a problem. If he led the king of clubs, declarer would trump it, after which the latter would undoubtedly (thought West) lay down the ace of trumps, catching West's now-singleton king. West's analysis of the situation was, of course, predicated on the evident fact that declarer couldn't reach the board to take a trump finesse. So West came up with a bit of neat thinking—he led *a low club* instead of the king, which declarer won with the board's ten-spot. On this trick, declarer discarded his jack of diamonds. It was now declarer's turn to do some thinking. His thought processes traversed this path: "I wonder why my capable West opponent led a low club, permitting me to win the trick in dummy, when he could have laid down his king of clubs, forcing me to ruff. He can see the dummy—and he darn well knows that I can't get there on my own power. It must be that he *wants* me to take a spade finesse—and if that's what *he* wants, it can't be right for me to take it. I'll bet my last dollar that he has the singleton king of trumps remaining. . . ."

Whereupon, a trump was led from dummy, declarer put up his ace, and caught West's singleton king. He thus made his doubled contract, losing two hearts and two diamonds.

Had West led the king of clubs instead of a low club, South would have ruffed. He would then have had no choice but to lead the spade ace, dropping West's king, after which he would have trumped his jack of diamonds to fulfill his contract.

As any potential victim can tell you, it is quite a feat to extricate oneself from the embrace of a boa constrictor once the latter has begun his process of entwinement. By analogy, with respect to the world of nonexpert bridgeplayers, escaping from an impending endplay being woven by an expert is well-nigh impossible.

The primary reason for the nonexpert's inability to escape is that he does not see the endplay coming; whereas the expert, having encountered similar situations in the past, can see and/or sense it coming, and is able to avoid its clutches. Here are two examples.

Deal 15:

Milton C. Work, who passed away in 1934, was the outstanding American authority on auction bridge. He was also a noted player in contract bridge. In his later years, he received the accolade of "The Grand Old Man of Bridge." In 1965 he was elected to bridgedom's Hall of Fame.

One of the deals of which he was most proud (and justifiably so) was the following, in which he escaped being the victim of an endplay. He used this deal frequently in his teaching of advanced players, for it illustrates not only agile defender's play, but also beautiful planning and preparation by declarer. Mr. Work was the West defender.

Neither side vulnerable. North dealer.

North

♠ 6 5 4 2
♡ J 6 5 2
◇ A Q 7
♣ 8 5

West

♠ A K Q 10 9 8 3
♡ —
◇ K J 2
♣ K J 10

East

♠ J 7
♡ 7
◇ 10 9 8 4
♣ 9 7 6 4 3 2

South

♠ —
♡ A K Q 10 9 8 4 3
◇ 6 5 3
♣ A Q

The bidding:

North	East	South	West
Pass	Pass	4 ♡	4 ♠
5 ♡	Pass	Pass	5 ♠
Pass	Pass	6 ♡	Double
Pass	Pass	Pass	

Mr. Work opened the spade king, and as South viewed the dummy, his first thought was probably: "West almost certainly has all of the outstanding high cards. I'm going to proceed on that assumption."

Whereupon South ruffed the opening lead with the queen of trumps and led the eight of hearts to dummy's jack. He next trumped another spade with the king of trumps. To trick four he led the three of trumps to dummy's five, after which he ruffed a third spade. A diamond was now led, and a winning finesse of the queen was taken. The board's last spade was then ruffed, and the stage was set to play the ace of diamonds, followed by another diamond, putting West into the lead.

West would now have no options but to lead 1.) a club, enabling declarer to win two club tricks or 2.) a spade or a diamond (the latter in theory), which declarer would trump in dummy, while simultaneously discarding his losing queen of clubs. But, en route, something had happened that prevented declarer from bringing his plan to fruition.

When declarer had led a diamond at trick six, finessing dummy's queen, Mr. Work had followed suit with his *jack* of diamonds, not the deuce. And two tricks later, when South had made a second lead of diamonds to the board's ace, Mr. Work had played his *king* of diamonds. And so it came to pass that when a third round of diamonds was led, *East* won the trick with his ten-spot. East, quite naturally, then led a club, enabling Mr. Work to cash the setting trick in that suit.

Mr. Work had perceived quite early in the play what the future held in store for him if he played normally and mechanically. When declarer had trumped the opening spade lead, and had then entered dummy at trick two to trump a second spade, Mr. Work saw the handwriting on the wall. His thoughts undoubtedly took this direction:

"There is no doubt in my mind that South, for his bidding, has the A Q of clubs and is trying to set me up for an endplay: to get me to lead away from my club king. He hopes to achieve this by throwing me into the lead with a diamond. He is making the essential preparation by ruffing out dummy's spades; and when he accomplishes this, I will be unable to exit safely by leading a spade, for the latter lead will permit dummy to ruff while declarer gets rid of a losing club. My only hope of preventing declarer from achieving his objective is to assume that my partner has the diamond ten; if he has it, then I can counterattack successfully. Without the diamond ten in my partner's hand, I am doomed to defeat."

And so Mr. Work jettisoned the jack and king of diamonds—and when East's ten of diamonds appeared on the third lead of the suit, it was a gorgeous sight to behold.

Deal 16:

By a strange coincidence, a deal bearing a remarkable similarity to the preceding one (with Milton Work in the West seat) came up some twenty-five years later. Actually, I suppose it really isn't too strange: with millions and millions of deals being played each year, coincidences and resemblances are to be expected.

Sitting West was the late Joseph Cohan, of Wooster, Ohio. The deal arose in 1957 in a Chicago Regional Pair Championship.

This is the deal:

East-West vulnerable. South dealer.

North

♠ J 9 7 5
♡ 8 6
◇ A 5 3
♣ 8 6 3 2

West

♠ 6 3
♡ K J 9 3
◇ Q J 2
♣ A K J 10

East

♠ 2
♡ 10 7 5 4 2
◇ 10 7 6 4
♣ 9 7 5

South

♠ A K Q 10 8 4
♡ A Q
◇ K 9 8
♣ Q 4

The bidding:

South	West	North	East
1 ♠	Double	2 ♠	Pass
4 ♠	Pass	Pass	Pass

Joe, on lead against South's four-spade contract, cashed his two top clubs and then led the club jack. Declarer, also an expert, did not hurriedly trump and then pause for examination. He examined first. Here is the gist of his thinking:

"Based on West's original double, my heart finesse is just about certain to lose—West surely has the heart king. But if I can get West to lead a heart to me, I'm home. My best bet is to ruff out dummy's fourth club and throw West into the lead with a diamond (West, rather than East, figures to have the diamond queen). He'll now be compelled to lead a heart—or a diamond, which will be equally acceptable, since I won't have any diamonds left in either hand—and my contract will be assured. Here goes."

West's lead of the jack of clubs at trick three was trumped by South, who then led the ten of spades and overtook it with dummy's jack. The board's remaining club was now ruffed with declarer's ace. The king of trumps was cashed next, felling West's outstanding trump.

Declarer then led his eight of diamonds toward dummy's ace. Joe, perceiving what declarer was trying to accomplish, covered the eight with his jack, dummy's ace winning. The three of diamonds now followed, and declarer put up his king. On this trick, Joe dropped the queen!

Declarer's remaining diamond was now put on the table, upon which Joe played the deuce, East capturing the trick with his ten-spot. East, of course, returned a heart, and West's king took the setting trick.

It is quite obvious that if West hadn't "unblocked" with the jack and queen of diamonds, he would have been forced into the lead on the third round of that suit. He would then have had no choice but to lead a heart, giving declarer a "free finesse" and a present of the heart queen.

Joe's comment—or, perhaps, criticism—on this deal was about declarer's line of play:

"If declarer, *at trick four,* had led a diamond to the ace, I'm not one hundred percent sure that I would have put up my jack.* At this early stage, I might not have seen what was coming. But when declarer led a trump to dummy's jack at trick four, and ruffed the

* I'm sure he would have.

board's last club, I was right there with him—he had opened my eyes. From here on my defense was a routine matter."

"Routine," he says. I'll accept it if he accepts that driving a racing car at 160 mph at the Indianapolis Speedway is as routine a matter as driving a mass-production standard American car at 60 mph over one of our superhighways. The mass-production car is built for comfort and relaxation. The racing car for maximum efficiency under extreme pressures.

Deal 17:

For those who are of the opinion that women can't become top-flight players because they don't possess the spur-of-the-moment imagination essential to top-echelon play, the following deal is submitted in refutation. It features some magnificent, highly imaginative defense by two of the West Coast's top players: Nell Wells and the late Ivy Oeschger. The deal arose in a sectional Womens Pair Championship held in California in 1950.

Neither side vulnerable. West dealer.

North
♠ 10 6 5 2
♡ A K 10 9 8
◇ Q 7
♣ 10 9

West
♠ A J 8 7
♡ Q J 7
◇ A 10 8 6
♣ 7 5

East
♠ K Q
♡ 6 4 2
◇ J 9 5 4 3 2
♣ J 4

South
♠ 9 4 3
♡ 5 3
◇ K
♣ A K Q 8 6 3 2

The bidding:

West	North	East	South
1 ♢	1 ♡	2 ♢	3 ♣
Pass	Pass	3 ♢	4 ♣
Pass	Pass	Pass	

The reader, in viewing the defense, should appreciate that this deal was played before "suit-preference" signals had become adopted by virtually all experts.*

Sitting in the West seat was Ivy Oeschger, and East was Nell Wells.

West opened the ace of diamonds, the seven was played from dummy, and quick as a flash Nell dropped the nine-spot. Now it was perfectly obvious to her that declarer had a singleton king of diamonds before declarer played that card to the first trick! After all, West had opened the bidding with one diamond, and in those days when you opened with one diamond you guaranteed at least four cards in the suit. (How different today, with the "short" club and "short" diamond bids!) And, further, when West had led the diamond ace, she could not have possessed the king, for with both of these top cards the king would have been opened. Hence, Ivy figured that Nell knew that South was going to play the king on the opening diamond lead.

Why on earth (said West to herself) is my partner playing the nine of diamonds on my opening lead? She knows that dummy's queen is high—and surely she doesn't want me to continue diamonds, for if I did it would enable declarer to discard a loser from her hand. Certainly the nine of diamonds is a signal for me *not* to lead diamonds. Obviously, it can't be a heart lead that my partner wants, what with the dummy having the ace and king. It must be, therefore, that my partner is trying to tell me to lead spades. For her to desire ("command" would perhaps be the better word) spades, she must possess the king of spades, if not both the king and the queen.

* The suit-preference signal is discussed in Chapter 12, pp. 234–38.

And so, having the utmost confidence in her partner, Ivy now led the seven of spades, underleading her ace! This lead was taken by Nell's king,* after which she played her queen. The inverse plays of the king and the queen in that order was unorthodox, and deliberately so, the hope being to get West to recognize that there was a purpose to it, namely to show a doubleton K Q.

Ivy (West) didn't miss the significance. She promptly overtook the spade queen with her ace, and cashed the spade jack, for the setting trick.

It is apparent that if Ivy had led either the spade ace at trick two, or had failed to overtake her partner's spade queen, declarer would have fulfilled her contract by discarding her losing spade on the board's established queen of diamonds. . . . "Oh, to be in England now that April's there. . . ."

* Normally, on defense, when you are third hand, you play the lower of two touching honors, and the lowest of three or more touching honors.

chapter **12**

THE TRIUMPH OF KNOWLEDGE

In the great majority of deals presented in this text, depicting the functioning of the expert mind, the emphasis has been on spur-of-the-moment, imaginative play. From the expert's point of view, the faculty of being able to bring his imagination into practical application when necessity so demands is one of the attributes that differentiates him from the nonexperts.

But, basically, the primary reason why experts are such consistent winners is that they possess great technical knowledge and skill in both bidding and play. With respect to bidding, they have assimilated all of the artificial, conventional (and, sometimes, most complicated) bids that figure to arise at various intervals during their lifetime, and have made them a component part of their arsenal of offensive and defensive weapons. Through this arsenal, they are enabled to handle with optimum effect almost every bidding situation that will confront them. With respect to play, our experts have run across virtually every type of situation involving the play of the cards, have learned to handle each of them instinctively and correctly, and have earmarked them for future reference and utilization.

The nonexpert, on the other hand, has not had these cumulative experiences in play, nor has he had the time or inclination to study and master the dozens of "fancy" bids which are essential to the expert's survival in a world of experts. As a result, the nonexpert is frequently forced to work out (or guess) at the bridge table the various bidding and play situations which the expert has previously encountered; which, in play, the expert knows by rote; and which, in bidding, the expert, with partner's concurrence, has incorporated into *their* "system."

Since one does not have unlimited time during the progress of a game to work out solutions (nor can he ask, during the bidding: "Partner, are we using the Flint Convention?"), the nonexpert is much more apt to err in, or misjudge or misinterpret, certain circumstances than is the knowledgeable expert.

Here are six deals that the expert would handle automatically and correctly as a result of his past experiences in analogous situations; while the nonexpert would either mishandle them or, via luck or a good guess, would reach home safely and happily.

These deals, all of which arose in toplevel duplicate games or in major tournaments, are concerned with bidding conventions, play conventions (defensive), and mathematical knowledge, the latter being derived from experience and not from books. Also, and foremost, the application of judgment based on knowledge accumulated through the years via repetitive situations always forms the expert's first line of offense, or defense, as the case might be.

Deal 1:

The story is told of the four brothers who were playing bridge in their hotel suite. Brother East opened the bidding with one club, Brother South overcalled with one notrump, Brother West passed, and Brother North bid three notrump. Brother East, the possessor of the six top clubs and the king of spades, doubled with gusto. Everybody then passed, after which Brother West opened—a heart!

Brother East was furious at Brother West because the latter had failed to lead clubs, East's bid suit. Brother East rose from the table without a word, and threw his cards out of the sixth-story hotel window. Brother West rushed to that window and pushed himself halfway out.

Brother East grabbed him and yelled: "You did a terrible thing by not leading my suit, but that's no reason to kill yourself!"

Brother West answered: "Who's trying to kill himself? I just wanted to see what kind of hand you had for your double."

With very few exceptions, when partner, after bidding a suit, has doubled the opponents for penalties in some contract, his double is a command for his suit to be led. One of the few exceptions arises when the opponents have arrived at a slam contract, in which case the double has a conventional, precise meaning: "Partner, forget my suit. *Lead the first suit bid by dummy.*"

Here is a classic illustration of the use of this conventional double against a slam contract. The deal arose in the 1965 Masters Pair Championship.

East-West vulnerable. North dealer.

North
♠ Q 4
♡ Q 6
◇ K Q 7
♣ A J 10 8 5 3

West
♠ J 7 6 5 2
♡ 9 8 4
◇ 3
♣ 9 7 6 4

East
♠ A K 10 9 8 3
♡ J 10 7 5 3 2
◇ 6
♣ —

South
♠ —
♡ A K
◇ A J 10 9 8 5 4 2
♣ K Q 2

The bidding:

North	East	South	West
1 ♣	1 ♠	3 ◇	Pass
4 ◇	Pass	7 ◇	Pass
Pass	Double	Pass	Pass
Pass			

West dutifully opened a club, dummy's first-bid suit, which East trumped for the setting trick. Had East not doubled, West would automatically have led a spade, East's bid suit, and declarer would have romped in with his grand-slam contract.

In retrospect, North-South could have made a grand slam in clubs, as North pointed out, sadly, after the diamond grand-slam contract had been defeated. Such is life.

Deal 2:

It was stated at the outset of this chapter that experts have at their disposal dozens of conventional and artificial bids that they can employ when the occasion so demands; whereas the nonexpert, unfamiliar with these gadgets, is forced to rely on guesswork when previously unencountered bidding situations arise.

The preceding deal illustrated one of these conventions: the double of a slam contract as calling for the lead of the first suit bid by dummy. This deal presents another artificial, conventional type of bid.

Both sides vulnerable. South dealer.

North

♠ 5 3 2
♡ A 7 4
◇ 6 2
♣ A K Q 10 3

West	**East**
♠ K 4	♠ A
♡ J 10 9 5 2	♡ K Q 8 6 3
◇ 10 7	◇ 8 5 3
♣ 9 8 6 5	♣ J 7 4 2

South

♠ Q J 10 9 8 7 6
♡ —
◇ A K Q J 9 4
♣ —

The bidding:

South	West	North	East
5 ♠	Pass	Pass	Pass

In the hands of the expert, the proper North-South contract of five spades is arrived at in one bid. In the hands of the nonexpert, in all probability a hopeless, unmakable slam would be reached; or even if the slam were not reached, South would anxiously await the appearance of the dummy to see whether a slam was or was not in the cards.

In nonexpert circles, South would undoubtedly open the bidding with two spades, forcing to game. North, having a magnificent responding hand, could then surely push on to at least a small slam, in either spades or notrump. As is apparent, any slam contract is doomed to defeat.

In expert circles, South would open the bidding with a conventional five-in-a-major opening, in this case "five spades." An opening bid of five in a major states: "Partner, if you have either the ace or king of my suit, bid a small slam in my suit. If you have both of these cards, bid a grand slam in my suit. *And if you have neither of these cards,* no matter what the rest of your hand is, PASS!"

Thus, on the above deal, South would open with five spades, which would become the final contract.

Quite obviously, hands such as South's do not come up too often. But, on occasion, they do arise—and when they do, the knowledgeable expert is a winner, while the nonexpert is a loser.

• • •

Deal 3:

This deal arose in the 1964 Spingold Team-of-Four Championships and features a necessary mathematical situation for unmathematical minds.

East-West vulnerable. South dealer.

North

♠ 7 4
♡ Q 10 9 7 3
◊ 5 4 2
♣ 8 7 5

West

♠ Q J 9 5 2
♡ K 6 4 2
◊ 9 7 3
♣ K

East

♠ K 10 8 6 3
♡ A J 8 5
◊ 6
♣ A 10 2

South

♠ A
♡ ——
◊ A K Q J 10 8
♣ Q J 9 6 4 3

The bidding:

South	West	North	East
2 ◊	Pass	2 NT	Pass
3 ♣	Pass	3 ◊	Pass
4 ♣	Pass	4 ◊	Pass
5 ◊	Pass	Pass	Pass

It might be noted, by the way, that East-West could have fulfilled a five-spade contract. But East, vulnerable, was reluctant to step into the bidding at the three-level in the face of a strong two-bid by South.

Against the five-diamond contract, West opened the queen of spades, South's ace winning. Trumps were then extracted in three rounds, after which declarer led the three of clubs. West took this with his singleton king, and returned a spade, declarer ruffing. The queen of clubs now drove out East's ace. The remainder of the tricks belonged to declarer, since the club suit had become established.

I could be wrong, but I imagine that virtually every inexpert declarer, after drawing trumps, would then have led the queen of clubs (losing to West's king). There would now have been no way to avoid the loss of two more club tricks to East's A 10, resulting in the defeat of the five-diamond contract.

Our declarer happened to be Arthur Robinson of Philadelphia, one of our nation's bridge internationalists. From his point of view (with mathematics to back him up), if either of the opponents had the A K 10 or the A K 10 2 of clubs, his contract was doomed, since in this case he would be compelled to lose three club tricks no matter what club he led; and if the four adversely held clubs were divided 2–2, it also made no difference what he played, since two leads of clubs would pick up the outstanding clubs with the loss of only two tricks.

But if the four outstanding clubs were divided 3–1, then the vital question was whether the singleton was the ace, the king, or the ten. If it were the ten-spot, then the initial lead of the club queen would fell the ten, resulting in the loss of just two club tricks (to the ace and king). But if the singleton were the ace or king, then the lead of the queen would result in the loss of three club tricks (as in the actual deal).

Mathematically (and logically), if the clubs were divided 3–1, the ten would be a singleton just one time out of four (i.e., one card out of four: A K, *10*, 2). The ace *or* king would be a singleton two times out of four (i.e., two cards out of four: *A*, *K*, 10, 2). Hence, the chances of *either* a singleton king *or* a singleton ace existing were twice as good as the chances of a singleton ten existing.

Hence, Robinson's play of a low club (rather than the queen) was made in the full knowledge that his play would gain more often than it would lose, with no guarantees on any given deal. In bridge parlance, his play is what is called a "percentage play."

To the nonexpert, the "suit-preference" signal is only a phrase. To the expert, this signal is a most practical weapon which frequently pinpoints the way to winning defensive play.

The suit-preference signal is used on defense when a player wishes his partner to switch suits. This signal eliminates a guess as to which of *two suits* partner should play. The reference to "two suits" may appear to be a typographical error. Actually, it is not. Of the four suits, the trump suit is automatically eliminated, for whenever partner gives any signal whatsoever, it is never to direct the lead of a trump suit. Also, the suit that is being led, on which the suit-preference signal is being given, is excluded. That leaves the leader with a choice of the two remaining suits.

Stating the suit-preference signal as a principle, it comes to this: "Whenever partner plays an *unnecessarily high card* that is obviously not a "come-on-in-this-suit" signal, it commands the leader to lead the higher of the two self-evident suits; whenever partner plays a very low card that is *obviously* not a "no-interest-in-this-suit" signal, that card asks partner to shift to the lower of the two self-evident suits. If the partner of the leader has no interest in either of the two self-evident suits, he will play some intermediate card in the suit being led.

Here are two illustrations of the suit-preference signal in action.

• • •

Deal 4:

Both sides vulnerable. North dealer.

North

♠ K Q J 2
♡ K 6
◊ K Q 10 7
♣ 8 6 3

West

♠ 3
♡ A 10 8 5
◊ 8 5 4 3 2
♣ 10 5 2

East

♠ 6
♡ Q J 7 4 3 2
◊ A 9 6
♣ 9 7 4

South

♠ A 10 9 8 7 5 4
♡ 9
◊ J
♣ A K Q J

The bidding:

North	East	South	West
1 ◊	Pass	1 ♠	Pass
2 ♠	Pass	6 ♠	Pass
Pass	Pass		

The fact that South failed to employ the Blackwood Slam Convention when it properly should have been employed, is immaterial to this discussion. Nonexpert bidding, such as the above, probably happens every day in every bridge club in the country. And I am certain that in a fair proportion of deals such as this, the defense slips, and declarer "steals" his unmakable contract.

As a matter of fact, when this deal arose in a duplicate game many years ago, South fulfilled his contract. West opened the ace of hearts, which won the trick, East following with the deuce. At that time, the suit-preference signal was just a theory, and West was at a loss as to what to play next. He decided to shift to a club, and declarer waltzed in with his contract, discarding his losing jack of diamonds on dummy's king of hearts.

With the employment of the suit-preference signal, the defense becomes routine. On the lead of the ace of hearts, East would toss his queen. *Obviously,* in the face of the dummy, this play could not be construed as asking for a heart continuation, and would be asking for a shift to the higher of the two remaining suits, diamonds as against clubs. A diamond lead would then be made at trick two, and declarer's slam contract would be defeated.

Had East held the ace of clubs instead of the ace of diamonds, he would have played the deuce of hearts on the opening lead, calling for a club lead, the lower of the two obvious suits. And, had East held no high cards in either diamonds or clubs, he would have played an intermediate heart—either the seven or the four—which would say to partner, "No interest in anything. You are on your own."

Deal 5:

The bidding on this deal is presented below as it actually occurred in a major tournament. After a slow start, the tempo picked up rapidly, with South reaching a good five-club contract that would have been fulfilled had East not employed a drastic and dramatic suit-preference signal.

North-South vulnerable. West dealer.

North
♠ Q 7 3
♡ 9
◇ K J 10 9 6
♣ 9 8 5 3

West
♠ A J 10
♡ A Q 8 6 4 3
◇ Q 7 2
♣ 6

East
♠ K 9 6 5 4 2
♡ 2
◇ 8 5 3
♣ J 7 2

South
♠ 8
♡ K J 10 7 5
◇ A 4
♣ A K Q 10 4

The bidding:

West	North	East	South
1 ♡	Pass	Pass	2 ♣
Pass	Pass	2 ♠	Pass
Pass	3 ♣	Pass	Pass
3 ♠	4 ♣	Pass	5 ♣
Pass	Pass	Pass	

West opened the ace of hearts, and East, who ardently desired a heart continuation (he could overruff dummy), had no choice but to play his lowly singleton deuce. To West (and to the world) this expressed a "no-interest-in-this-suit, partner" play. So, at trick two, West shifted to the ace of spades, the three-spot being played from dummy.

On this trick, East made a most dramatic play—he tossed the *king of spades!* With the spade queen in evidence in dummy, it did not require genius to recognize that East's tossing away of the highest spade left in the deck did not request a spade continuation. (It was even more obvious when one considers that East had voluntarily bid spades, and, hence, could not have had a singleton king.) Since East-West were employing the suit-preference signal, East's play of the king *demanded* that West lead the higher of the two *obvious* remaining suits: hearts versus diamonds.

So West dutifully played a heart, dummy ruffed with the nine, and East overruffed with the jack, for the setting trick.

Had East not played the spade king on West's lead of the ace at trick two, West *probably* (or, as I see it, "undoubtedly") would have continued spades, declarer ruffing. No matter how declarer now played the diamond suit (either by finessing West for the queen or by cashing the ace and king and trumping a third round), he would have fulfilled his contract.

It might be argued that even if East had played the deuce of spades at trick two, when West led the ace, signifying no interest in the spade suit, West might well have led a heart at trick three, enabling East to overruff dummy. Quite true. But the fact is that the play of the king of spades eliminated any guesswork on West's part—and those who can eliminate guesswork win more often than they lose.

It might also be argued that when East tossed away the king of spades, he might well have given declarer a present of a trick, which would have been the case if West, who had supported spades, had four spades instead of three. Declarer, in this case, would have been void of spades. But, from the East seat, even if the queen of spades were promoted into a winner, it wouldn't help declarer, for the diamond suit in dummy figured to provide declarer with all the winners he needed to fulfill his game contract.

Deal 6:

It has been said—with validity—that experts frequently play out a hand as though they are able to see through the backs of the opponents' cards, and know exactly what each one is holding. I vouch for the correctness of that statement. However, their seeming "clairvoyance" is not the result of an innate attribute, but is due, rather, to a proper interpretation of the clues that are in evidence to the discerning eye and ear.

Here is a deal where the ear—listening to an opponent's bid—guided declarer to the plausible and winning line of play. The deal arose in a regional tournament held in Philadelphia in 1953. The South declarer was the late Sidney Silodor, world-renowned internationalist.

Neither side vulnerable. South dealer.

North

♠ J 7 3 2
♡ K 10 6 3
◇ 8 4
♣ 10 7 3

West

♠ K 10 8
♡ A 8 4
◇ A K 10 5
♣ Q 6 4

East

♠ 9 6 5 4
♡ —
◇ J 9 7 6 3 2
♣ 8 5 2

South

♠ A Q
♡ Q J 9 7 5 2
◇ Q
♣ A K J 9

The bidding:

South	West	North	East
1 ♡	1 NT	2 ♡	3 ◇
4 ♡	Pass	Pass	Pass

With respect to the bidding, West's one-notrump overcall denoted an opening bid of one notrump (16–18 high-card points). North's raise to two hearts indicated a poor hand with trump support (with a decent hand, North would have made a penalty double).

Against the four-heart contract West opened the king of diamonds, after which he continued with the ace, Silodor ruffing. The jack of trumps was then led, West and North following with low ones, with East discarding a diamond. Another trump was next led by South, West taking his ace and returning a trump, dummy's king winning. Here is the way Sidney justified his line of play from here in:

"I had 19 high-card points, and my dummy had 4. West, for his notrump overcall, had 16–18. Therefore West, for his overcall, had to have *both the king of spades and the queen of clubs.* Without both of these cards, West could not have had 16 high-card points.

"Thus if I took both the spade and club finesses, each of them was certain to lose. But if I could throw West into the lead with a club and force him to lead a spade, or, instead, throw him into the lead with a spade and compel him to lead a club, then I could restrict my losses in the black suits to just one trick. The burning question was, of course, with which suit should I throw him into the lead?*

"If I played the ace of spades and then the queen, everything would be fine if West had started with the doubleton king of spades. In this case, he would now be compelled to lead either a club (which would give me a free finesse and enable me to trump my fourth club with dummy's last trump) or a diamond, which I would trump in my own hand while simultaneously discarding dummy's three of clubs.

"But if West had three or more spades, then when I threw him into the lead with the spade queen, he would simply exit with a spade, and wait for the setting trick with the queen of clubs. (On dummy's jack of spades, I would discard a club, but I would still have a club loser remaining.) I felt that the odds were distinctly against West having exactly the doubleton king of spades.

"If, on the other hand, West had been dealt *either* the Q x or Q x x of clubs, then I could guarantee my contract. And it was more

* If West, upon being thrust into the lead with either a spade or a club, chose to play back a diamond, South would trump it in dummy while simultaneously discarding his losing queen of spades, thus avoiding the loss of a spade trick.

logical—and, mathematically, more probable—that West had either the Q x or Q x x of clubs than for him to have precisely the K x of spades.

"Hence, after winning West's trump return with dummy's king (at trick five), I elected to play my ace and king of clubs. When the queen did not fall, I led my nine of clubs, West taking the trick with his queen. West had just become the victim of an endplay: if he led a spade, my queen would become a winner. And if he led a diamond instead, I would trump in dummy while discarding my losing queen of spades.

"Actually, he made the correct play of a low spade—hoping his partner possessed the queen—but his only reward was a clear conscience for having done the right thing."

ABOUT THE AUTHOR

Fred L. Karpin is the author of a number of successful bridge books that have sold well over half a million copies and include: *The Point-Count System of Bidding in Contract Bridge, The Play of the Cards, How to Play Slam Contracts,* and *Psychological Strategy in Contract Bridge;* he is also the co-author of *The Complete Book of Duplicate Bridge.* For a number of years, Mr. Karpin has been running very popular bridge classes in the Washington, D.C., area, the registration for which averages over 3000 students a year. He currently writes a bridge column for *The Washington Post,* shortly to be nationally syndicated through the Times-Mirror newspaper group, and is also a frequent contributor to the leading bridge magazines.